VELOCITY SELLING

VELOCITY SELLING

How to Attract,
Engage and Empower
Buyers to **BUY**

BOB URICHUCK

New York

VELOCITY SELLING

How to Attract, Engage and Empower Buyers to **BUY**

Published in New York, New York, by Morgan James Publishing. Morgan James and The Entrepreneurial Publisher are trademarks of Morgan James, LLC.
www.MorganJamesPublishing.com

ISBN 978-1-61448-817-0 paperback
ISBN 978-1-61448-818-7 eBook
ISBN 978-1-61448-819-4 audio
ISBN 978-1-61448-867-5 hardcover
Library of Congress Control Number:
2013945583

Editing by:
Karen Runtz

Cover Design by:
Rachel Lopez
www.r2cdesign.com

Interior Design by:
Bonnie Bushman
bonnie@caboodlegraphics.com

This book is dedicated to my late mother and father. Since I was a child they gave me the business opportunities to realize that the world revolves around sales. Sales is all about relationships. Relationships increase your network, and in turn, your net worth.

To my loving wife, Joan, and my wonderful sons, Michael and David, who have supported and encouraged me in all endeavors.

This book is also dedicated to those who have decided to improve their selling skills in order to increase their ROTI (return on time invested) and sales effectiveness, and to improve the quality of their lives and the lives of others with whom they come in contact.

TABLE OF CONTENTS

FOREWORD

by Brian Tracy, Author, *Unlimited Sales Success*

As you know, we all need sales to survive. But, we need buyers to make sales.

Once you understand how buyers buy and how they control the sales process, you will want to change how you conduct your sales. Buyers follow a system, and so should salespeople. The system must attract, engage and empower the buyer to buy especially considering today's new economy of buyers.

Allow me to introduce you to Bob Urichuck's "Buyer Focused" Velocity Selling System—a simple non-traditional step-by-step sales process that attracts, engages and empowers buyers to buy while increasing the velocity of your selling cycle, and your bottom line.

For the last fifteen years, using Singapore and Dubai as his ongoing hubs for Asia and the Middle East, Bob has personally worked with Fortune 500 companies and mid-size businesses in over forty-five countries, spending up to thirty days a year in the air, for those who had the budget to invest in hiring him.

Now he has made his Velocity Selling System accessible and affordable to all through this book and through his continuous learning, interactive video-based virtual sales training system at VelocitySelling.com.

I highly recommend the "Buyer Focused" Velocity Selling System and its step-by-step approach. It allows you to learn a step at a time, apply and master it in the real world, and come back and learn the next step. Affordable, accessible and continuous learning at its best.

The Velocity Selling System will help you attract, engage and empower more buyers, shorten your sales cycle, increase your margins and revenue and generate the bottom line results you are looking for, without the costs of travel, accommodation or costly sales trainers.

Velocity Selling is an easy and enjoyable read that will take you through the system in a simple A, B, C, D format. No matter if you are selling online, offline, over the telephone or face-to-face, you will learn the fundamentals of communications and human interaction. You will learn the importance of having a strong foundation upon which to build — **Attitude**. You will discover how daily **Behaviors** will lead to an increased bottom line, while getting you the best return on your time. You will then learn the **Competencies** of the "Buyer Focused" Velocity Selling System and end with your well-defined **Disciplines** that will keep you on top of realizing your goals — personally and professionally.

With all the manipulative sales techniques removed from the process, you will experience stronger buyer relationships, faster sales cycles, higher margins and profits, and improved closing ratios. You will have more satisfied customers and more referrals. Ultimately you will Up Your Bottom Line in weeks, not months.

Velocity Selling is a must-read for sales professionals — independents and corporate sales teams, entrepreneurs, business owners, non-selling professionals and anyone who wants to learn from the foundation up how to be in control of the sales process, shorten sales cycles, be sought after, make more money and much, much more...

The time has come. Enjoy the learning!

PREFACE

Sales are flatlined, buyers are slow to buy, sales cycles are too long, control of the sales process has been lost, the bottom line is behind projections…

Most organizations today are aware that the economy has brought on a shift from selling during the boom times to attracting, engaging and empowering the new economy of buyers to buy.

One absolute fact is that the traditional and consultative sales methods no longer work. While these methods still work in certain selling situations, it's becoming increasingly clear that their effectiveness is waning. The sales cycle is longer than need be and margins are dropping.

Buyers have been educated by salespeople regarding all imaginable sales techniques. As a result, salespeople have taught buyers everything they know and buyers have developed a process to counteract the actions of salespeople.

Unfortunately, salespeople don't even realize they have lost control. The buyers are in control of the interaction during the sales process, not the salespeople.

Over time, buyers became appalled by our high-pressure tactics, sleazy sales gimmicks and manipulative closing techniques. And as information became easier to gather and to evaluate via the internet, they gained more control.

Buyers today can purchase whatever they want, whenever they want and without a salesperson confronting them and taking up their valuable time. The top buyer complaint about salespeople, and I quote, is "they waste my time."

In fact, in the past five years, the emerging power and accessibility of information over the web has finally tipped the scales of power to the buyer. The buyers are in control.

In order to succeed in sales you need to do the opposite of selling. You need to attract, engage and empower buyers to buy.

The sales process has to be transformed into a no-pressure exchange where "getting to the truth" and building a relationship is the goal. It becomes more important to bring in the right buyers for the right reasons instead of simply making a sales pitch or even a sale.

If you truly and sincerely want to be the problem solver, then do away with the traditional or consultative approach with today's new economy of buyers.

Sales has been a way of life for me since I was a boy. I was raised in a small family business and, thanks to both of my late parents, I was exposed to the world of sales. You may say I was raised to be in sales and for that I am really grateful.

After graduating from college with honors in business administration, I got involved in multi-level and network marketing, became a door-to-door salesperson, and then later joined a major oil corporation in a sales and marketing capacity. I had a passion for land development and started developing and selling land. I then got involved with the majors—some of the world's leading land developers and builders—in mass sales and large-price boardroom selling.

Up until that point I had no formal sales training, but I realized that the world revolved around sales, although it was not and is still not a well-respected profession. I intend to change that perception to one of high respect and recognition.

Later in life, while working with a major corporation, I positioned myself into their newly formed sales training department. I had to come up with a sales training program within one year. During that year, I attended over thirty of the world's top sales training programs. While I was doing my job and recommending a program to the organization, I also did a best-practice analysis and created the "Buyer Focused" Velocity Selling System.

For over fifteen years now, I have trained business owners, entrepreneurs, selling and non-selling professionals and organizations of all sizes in a variety of industries—from leading airlines to automobiles, banking, insurance, investments, real estate, pharmaceuticals, hotels and resorts, tourism, high-end jewelry, high technology, oil and gas, media, transportation, to major learning institutions, associations and government departments in over forty-five countries—on the "Buyer Focused" Velocity Selling System. The system has proven itself on bottom-line results time and time again and gained me recognition as one of the World's Top 5 Sales Gurus. It is now your turn to learn all about it.

The "Buyer Focused" Velocity Selling System

STEP-BY-STEP OVERVIEW

In order to succeed in sales, you need to do the opposite of selling. You must attract, engage and empower buyers to buy. Without buyers, there are no sales.

The bottom line: no buyers, no sales, no revenue. Sales now revolve around buyers. Buyers are everywhere. What are you doing to help them buy?

Once you understand how buyers buy and how they control the sales process, you will want to change how you conduct your sales. Buyers follow a system, and so should salespeople. The system must attract, engage and empower the buyer to buy, especially considering today's new economy of buyers.

The "Buyer Focused" Velocity Selling System is a sales process based on a return on time invested (ROTI) formula. With all the manipulative sales techniques and upfront presentations removed from the process, salespeople experience stronger client relationships, faster sales cycles, higher margins and profits, and improved closing ratios. You will have more satisfied customers, more attraction, more introductions and referrals, and a much improved bottom line.

The "Buyer Focused" Velocity Selling System is not a quick fix. It is not about better sales techniques and tricks to manipulate a prospect. It is honest, ethical and buyer-focused, which requires a different mindset, not only for the salesperson but for their management as well.

The new economy of selling is about buyers. The "Buyer Focused" Velocity Selling™ System ensures that you and/or your sales team are engaged in a step-by-step process to take ownership. The result: They Execute the Disciplines of Attracting, Engaging and Empowering the Velocity Selling Cycle, to Up Your Bottom Line.

Learning the "Buyer Focused" Velocity Selling System is as simple as A, B, C, D.

It is crucial to your overall success that you begin with a strong foundation to support the productive behaviors and the appropriate competencies within the Velocity Selling System.

A. You can't build anything without a solid foundation. The **"A"** is for **Attitude: Belief from Within**—the foundation of all successful people.

There are three steps in this category:

1. Attitude Toward YOU

This is the foundation to success, as everything revolves around you and your attitude toward yourself. You will learn how to take hold of your attitude, realize it is yours and develop an attitude of self-respect and self-confidence. You will discover what is holding you back and how to overcome fear. You will realize what is within your control and what is not. You will get to know who you really are, from the inside out, and how to be the best you can be.

2. Attitude Toward Your Organization

You will reflect, confirm and take hold of your attitude toward your organization, its products and services, and fellow team members. You will develop an owner's mentality and aim to improve. You will know how to identify your successes and become proactive in all that you do, while contributing to team effectiveness.

3. Attitude Toward Your Buyers

You will reflect, confirm and take hold of your win-win attitude as it pertains to the market and its buyers. You will realize that perceptions usually become reality and you will define the perceptions you want buyers to have of you. In turn, you will demonstrate a captivating attitude. You will also learn how to analyze and evaluate the competition in your market and use that information to your advantage.

A positive attitude alone is not enough to guarantee long-term success. Goals and an action plan are needed to get you where you want to go—they are the bottom line to success.

The **"B"** is for **Behavior: Your Bottom Line**-—the daily actions that are required to accomplish goals.

The three steps in this category are:

1. Behavior Toward Yourself

You will learn on your own personal level to understand the relationship between consistent positive behaviors and success. You will identify and develop personal goals and action plans based on your desires, while creating permanent self-motivation. As you learn to accept a new positive behavior toward yourself, you will become more successful in all that you do.

2. Behavior Toward Organization

You will follow the same procedures to develop goals, action plans and behaviors for organizational objectives as you did for personal goals. You will learn how to track your behaviors to understand and improve on your "call-to-close" ratio. You will learn how to treat your job as your business and to develop an owner's mentality and be proactive, not reactive. You will learn how to take control of your daily pay-time and no-pay-time behaviors and to focus on your time management skills. The bottom-line results, in numbers, come from demonstrating the appropriate behaviors, which you will define in this process.

3. Behavior Toward Your Buyers

By focusing your sales efforts through the 80/20 rule and the Velocity Selling A, B, C buyer target model, you will discover your best ROTI—return on time invested. You will learn and create "retain" and "regain" buyer strategies. You will learn and create a "gain" strategy using a personal marketing plan that will position you as an expert in your marketplace and attract the right buyers for your products or services. In other words, you will have buyers chasing you and you will never have to chase buyers again!

You now have a new and improved attitude and goal-driven behaviors. Now it is time to discuss the "C," which stands for **Competencies: the "Buyer Focused" Velocity Selling.** Just like any other professional—a doctor or lawyer, for instance—a sales professional requires certain competencies.

In this section, you are going to learn the required competencies to be in control of the sales process and to be a success in sales whether your communications with a buyer are conducted face-to-face, by the telephone, by networking, or via e-mail.

Competencies is divided into two parts:

In **Part 1** you will learn how buyers buy and what universal needs all buyers have. Then you will learn the three major competencies that you need to master first:

1. How to be buyer-focused to gain trust and shorten the sales cycle.
2. How to engage buyers by learning and applying advanced questioning and listening techniques that will help you stay in control and keep the buyer engaged and talking.
3. How to empower the buyer to buy through self-discovery.

You will also learn the five positive outcomes to a sales call and how to use them to your advantage on every sales call.

In **Part 2** you will learn the four-step "Buyer Focused" Velocity Selling System step by step. This process has been tried and proven internationally in all kinds of industries, across varied goods and services, online, over the telephone and in face-to-face situations.

Without the required competencies of the "Buyer Focused" Velocity Selling system, time is wasted, sales cycles are longer, margins are poor and there are no meaningful bottom-line results.

The four steps that you will learn to master are:

1. Building Relationships

Sales is a process. The first step of the Velocity Selling System is to build rapport to gain the buyer's trust. Without trust, nothing will happen.

You will learn techniques on how to build rapport in the first thirty seconds of meeting someone, allowing you to start a relationship with velocity.

2. Qualifying Buyer Opportunities

You will learn how to know when rapport has been established and to transition into step 2. You will learn how to initiate qualifying buyer opportunities by engaging the buyer into setting parameters or ground rules for the interaction, putting the buyer at ease and eliminating surprises. You will learn how to use your new questioning techniques to uncover the buyer's buying motivators, his/her financial ability, and the decision-making hierarchy, and to then summarize your findings to determine whether or not you can help the buyer. This process lets you qualify the buyer at a much deeper level, organizationally and personally, prior to making a proposal or presentation, allowing you to shorten your sales cycle and generate better ROTI—return on time invested.

3. Prescribing Solutions

In this step you will learn how to prescribe solutions in proposal and/or presentation formats that are specific to the identified buying motivators, financial ability and decision-making capabilities. You will learn the importance of the rule to "sell today, and educate tomorrow" and how you can give the buyer more value, leading to more word-of-mouth referrals.

You will also learn how to empower the buyer to buy; how to deal upfront with potential back outs, such as buyer's remorse and competitors; and how to ask for referrals.

4. Maintaining Buyer Relationships

Now that the buyer has purchased your prescribed solution, you will learn how to educate the buyer and give them additional value, while creating a secondary sales force of new buyer introductions and referrals. In addition, you will learn how to maintain a solid long-term relationship, increasing your network and your net worth.

At this point of the learning, you should now have a new and improved attitude—based on beliefs from within, with bottom-line goal-driven proactive ROTI behaviors—and mastered the competencies of the "Buyer Focused" Velocity Selling System.

Now it is time to discuss the **"D,"** which stands for **Disciplines: Doing What You Have to Do**.

> *Discipline is the key to your success. Discipline is a commitment to the most important person in the world. It means doing what you have to do, even when you don't want to do it.*
>
> **—Bob Urichuck**

As you complete each of the previously mentioned categories and chapters, you have the opportunity to identify those daily, weekly and monthly disciplines that you need to put into action. Now it is time to gather and summarize these into your daily disciplines based on the following three steps.

1. Discipline Toward Yourself

Accept that you are the most important person in the world and that your first need is to take care of yourself. Everything in your life revolves around your self-esteem, your belief and your behavior toward yourself. What daily, weekly and monthly disciplines do you need to apply toward yourself and your future success?

2. Discipline Toward Organization

You realize why you are motivated about going to work and how each day brings you a day closer to the realization of your dreams. What daily, weekly and monthly disciplines do you need to apply toward reaching your sales success and organizational goals?

3. Discipline Toward Buyers

You defined and are modeling the perception you want from buyers. You conduct the appropriate pay-time and no-pay-time behaviors and you always strive for the best ROTI. You attract, engage and empower buyers to buy. What daily, weekly and monthly disciplines do you need to apply toward buyers to ensure the above becomes real?

THE UNDERSTANDING OF FOUR KEY WORDS

1. Success: From the Inside Out
2. Motivation: Internal vs. External
3. Discipline: Doing What You Have to Do
4. Attitude: Under Whose Control?

Before we go forward on this journey we must first understand what success, motivation, discipline, attitude and selling from within are all about.

1. SUCCESS: FROM THE INSIDE OUT

What does success mean to you?

This can be a difficult question because we often look to others as examples. We see the Smiths down the street with a beautiful home, a swimming pool and a new car. By the looks of things, we might consider the Smiths successful, since most people tend to base success on material possessions.

But are they, or is it just a front to try to impress the neighbors? For all we know, they could be unhappy, heavily in debt and hate what they are doing. So why do we judge people by their external appearances and material possessions and compare ourselves with their apparent success?

Is that what success is all about?

Success means different things to different people. The reality is, success means whatever *you* want it to mean.

To a salesperson, it could be a major client acquisition, qualifying for an incentive, making a predetermined annual income or commission, being recognized at the annual sales conference as salesperson or team player of the year, or simply meeting quota and maintaining a job. Each of us has different desires.

Don't compare yourself with others and what *they* think success means. Believe it or not, you are already successful in many different ways. You just haven't taken the time to realize it yet. I am sure you've succeeded in accomplishing many of the things you desired in life—learning to ride a bike, learning to read and write, graduating, buying a car or a home, finding the right person and getting married, having children, and so on. These are all desires, or goals, that you have accomplished.

You have succeeded so far in your life, haven't you?

Let's take a look at two couples. Peter and Mary dress really well, drive BMWs, live in a beautiful home and always appear to have money to spend.

Would you classify them as a success?

Based on the information provided, you probably would. But if we go behind the scenes, we discover that they are not happy in their jobs, they are in debt over their heads and their only goal is for one of their fathers to die so that they can inherit his money.

How many people do you know that live a life of "fake success"? They are living their life from the outside in.

Is this what success is all about?

Another couple, John and Sandra, appear a little different to society. John stays home and takes care of three children, while Sandra, a petite blond, leaves each morning with a metal lunch box and a hard hat and works in construction.

Would you classify them as a success?

Based on the information provided, you probably would not. But going behind the scenes, we discover that they are happy and each is living the life of their dreams.

When John was a child, his parents never seemed to be around. They were always busy at work or elsewhere. When John was a teenager, he set a goal for himself to be a parent and his dream was to stay home and raise children. Today, John stays home and parents full-time.

As for Sandra, she used to work in the corporate world with me, but always had a passion to get involved in high rise construction and leave landmarks around the world.

Is each partner doing what they want to be doing? Are they successful?

Do you think they care what society thinks of them?

Are they living their life from the outside in or the inside out?

Look back again at the two different ways we have looked at success. In the first example, we looked at success from an external point of view—we compared ourselves to others. In the second example, we considered success from an internal point of view, a view of our desires in life—and they don't have to concern money, power or material things. Your desire could be for a certain lifestyle, education, career, marriage or anything you want to have, be or do.

So, what is the definition of success?

Success is defined as the progressive realization of a worthy goal or desire.

The key is to determine your desires—not only in sales, but in life—then turn these desires into goals to be accomplished. Success, as defined above, is the progressive realization of a worthy goal or desire.

2. MOTIVATION, INTERNAL VS. EXTERNAL

Motivation is another word that needs to be understood. Many people attend motivational talks and seminars to get motivated.

All kinds of people attend my motivational events and I always ask them—"By a show of hands, how many of you think I can motivate you today?"

All the hands go up in the air. Then I tell the audience that they are in the wrong room, because I have learned a long time ago that I cannot motivate anybody.

Let's understand this: only I can motivate myself and only you can motivate yourself. All I can do is provide you with the ideas, concepts and tools. The final decision on what you do with these things is up to whom?

YOU! Only you can motivate you!

Do you agree?

It is desire and the envisioning of success that creates self-motivation. When you can see, feel and hear the outcome of your desire, you create the belief that it will happen. These expectations motivate you toward those images of success.

Motivation is a desire held in the expectation that it will be accomplished. It all starts with desire—having a burning passion for something. Without desire, you cannot be motivated. Once the desire has set in, you must see, hear and feel your dream—and be able to visualize it in detail as if it already exists. This is the only true form of motivation because it comes from inside you.

Motivation is a motive for action. We are motivated toward images of success, which we expect to provide us with pleasure and gain. At the same time, we are motivated to avoid failure, pain and loss. If we keep images of success, pleasure and gain in our mind, we will be motivated toward them. However, if we keep images of failure, pain and loss foremost in our mind, we will be motivated merely to stay away from them, or just not be motivated at all.

Unfortunately, so many people rely on *external motivators*, for example, lottery tickets and incentives. These many forms of external motivators have a problem—their effect doesn't last. As soon as you acquire an incentive, you'll want a bigger and better one. As soon as you face up to a threat, the threat will no longer stop you. External motivation is temporary, or never-lasting.

The only true form of motivation comes *from* you, *for* you. This is *internal motivation*—the only everlasting motivation.

Motivation is the ability to see, in the present, a projection of the future that you want for yourself.

How do you want to be motivated—externally or internally?

3. DISCIPLINE: DOING WHAT YOU HAVE TO DO

"Discipline is the key to success. Discipline is a commitment to the most important person in the world. It means doing what you have to do, even when you do not want to do it."

—Bob Urichuck

Discipline is a commitment, a pledge to your course of action whereby you take on the complete responsibility to "make things happen." There are no more excuses. This is no longer "I hope." This is putting one foot ahead of the other and doing it.

It is now time to make the biggest commitment you will ever make—a commitment to yourself, the most important person in the world.

For example—do you make New Year's resolutions? Do you manage to stick to them? If so, congratulations! You are part of a small and exceptional group. Most people give up on their "resolutions" within two to three weeks. They lack discipline!

We respect, and usually follow through on, our commitments to others. When it comes to commitments to ourselves, though, we often allow external influences to win. We give in. And to make it worse, we tend to give in just under the twenty-one-day mark when the habit could be broken, or the commitment could become habit.

Rather than recognizing the success we had while trying to keep the resolution, we dwell on the "what if I can't do it?"

Of all commitments, the ones you make to yourself are the most important to respect. If you can't keep a commitment to yourself, you can't succeed.

To commit to something is to take a risk. You must loosen your hold on what you know as certain and reach for the unknown that you believe is better than what you have.

It's natural to be afraid when you take a risk. You are venturing into the unknown. But if you don't take risks you will live a life without growth. You will have to give up something in order to move ahead, but avoiding risks is the surest way of losing.

You can succeed if your willingness to leap overpowers your concern about what could happen if you fail. Avoid the regret of looking back on a life of opportunities not taken. Take the chance and commit to accomplishing your dreams.

James Garner says it best: *"I don't know when to stop. When I make a commitment, it is to the end."*

Now answer this question for yourself: What is your most productive time of the day—morning, day or night?

What would happen if you dedicated one hour of your most productive time to the most important person in the world?

Determine your most productive time of the day and dedicate it to "me" time. "Me" time is for you to do whatever you have to do that will bring you closer to achieving your goals. It may be as simple as visualizing the accomplishment of your goals or doing what you have to do, for you.

The point is to dedicate at least one hour of the most productive time for the most important person in the world.

I used to wake up at 7 a.m. and have a coffee. When I realized I was a morning person, I changed the time I woke up to an hour earlier, 6 a.m.

By making it a daily discipline, rising earlier became a habit.

What a difference it made.

"Bob time," as I refer to my first hour of the day, is one of my most important daily disciplines. It allows me to focus on me—my needs, desires and direction. When Bob time is over, what do you think is my reward? Now, keep it simple.

The important point to remember here is that any reward that gets recognized or rewarded gets repeated.

I reward myself with my first cup of coffee. How much more do you think I enjoy that cup of coffee now? And while drinking that coffee I give thanks for being able to have one when there are millions of people in the world who cannot even get a clean glass of water.

But it doesn't end there. I like to stay fit, so the next hour is dedicated to walking, swimming or doing some form of physical exercise. When that hour is done, what do you think my reward is then?

Right, breakfast. And again I give thanks for being able to have breakfast when there are children in our neighborhoods who go to school without breakfast.

Now I want you to also think of the opposite. Let's pretend I stayed out late and slept in and got up late. If I reward myself for appropriate behavior, should I not also punish myself for inappropriate behavior?

If I miss out on Bob time or exercise, I punish myself. I do not have that cup of coffee or breakfast. Remember, any behavior that gets recognized or rewarded gets repeated. I only want to recognize and reward appropriate behaviors.

After completing my morning disciplines, I go to work. How do you think I feel?

Imagine, how can I, as a speaker/trainer, be effective in giving audiences messages, if I first don't give to myself? How can I give you something, if I don't have it inside to give away.

What messages do you have inside and what are you giving away during your day?

Start by identifying your most productive time of the day and dedicate it to the most important person in the world. When completed, reward yourself with something you enjoy.

I will share more on discipline with you in later chapters. For now, start with the discipline of "me" time and identify your rewards and punishment.

4. ATTITUDE, UNDER WHOSE CONTROL?

A. Characteristics of Successful Salespeople

So, what makes up a successful salesperson? Obviously, reaching their goals is one aspect, but let's have a close look at the characteristics of successful salespeople. What would you identify as the top ten characteristics of successful salespeople?

Over the years I have witnessed all kinds of responses. If I told you the ten most popular, would it make a difference to what you wrote? You would think you were right or wrong. But what you wrote is right. What you didn't write is wrong. Take the time and write out ten characteristics of successful salespeople based on what you have witnessed or desired for yourself.

Review your list. How many of these characteristics do you possess? How many of them do you want to possess? What must you do?

My intention is to help you to discover things for yourself. That is the only way that the learning will make a difference. Some of the characteristics that I hear regularly are the following: goal driven, focused, communicates well—asks a lot of questions and listens well, organized, follows through, persistent, patient, honest, trustworthy, professional at all times, presents well, dresses well, cares, able to solve problems, results-oriented, doesn't take rejection personally, is enthusiastic and passionate about their profession, product or service and the organization they represent.

Identify the characteristics that you already have and the ones that you need to work on. Each month, add one of the characteristics that you need to work on to your Monthly Monitor Chart (identified in "B" Behavior) and keep it identified on the chart until you have mastered that characteristic.

Note that to master each characteristic requires desire. Desire comes from your ________!

B. How do Buyers Like to Be Treated?

Now that we have identified some characteristics of successful salespeople, let's take a look from the other side of a sale—from the buyer's point of view. Think of the last time you purchased something from a salesperson. How were you treated? As a buyer, how would you like to be treated?

Like most buyers, you probably want to be treated fairly and honestly. You want to be acknowledged, listened to, understood, appreciated and valued, shown respect, made to feel important, made to feel comfortable. But, as you know, such treatment does not always happen when dealing with salespeople. How should you, as a professional salesperson, behave?

Let's take another look at the above list. Is the way you are treated based on the attitude, behavior or competency of a salesperson?

You can say all three are the basis for being treated in a certain way. For example, buyers like to be listened to. To listen to someone may be a competency, as you have heard of competent listeners. However, before becoming competent, one must practice listening—that is a behavior. But, before one can practice listening, they must first have a desire to want to listen, and desire comes from your ______!

C. What is the Key Success Factor?

So, where does it all start? With attitude! Attitude is the key success factor and the foundation to your success.

What is attitude? Attitude is your way of thinking or behaving. Your attitude toward people influences your behavior toward them. Your attitude affects your level of satisfaction with life and with your job. Your attitude affects everyone who comes into contact with you. Your attitude is reflected in your tone of voice, posture and facial expressions. Your attitude can affect your health. It is your attitude that will make the biggest difference in your life—particularly when it comes to sales. Your past and present are a result of your past attitude. However, your present attitude will determine your future. The greatest thing about attitude is that it is not fixed and it is 100 percent under your control. Your attitude is up to you!

Whether you think you can, or you think you can't, you're absolutely right.

—Henry Ford

Your attitude is created by your beliefs. Your beliefs were developed in your past. It may be time to re-evaluate them. Dig deep and make the necessary changes. Your present-day beliefs determine your attitude. It is your attitude that determines how you feel. How you feel determines how you act and how you act determines your results in the realization of your dream.

Your self-image, your self-worth, your self-esteem and your self-confidence are all part of your attitude. How others see or perceive you can influence your attitude, as it may have done in the past. That is external influence. If you accept that influence, whether it is positive or negative, you will let it affect you internally. However, if you become aware of those external influences and decide to lead from within, you can refuse to let them affect you. In this way, you start to take control of your attitude, and your life.

It all starts within you, from within the most important person in the world. You have to sell yourself on you, before you can sell anything to anybody.

ATTITUDE: BELIEF FROM WITHIN

ATTITUDE TOWARD *YOU*

Who is the most important person in the world? Who is your greatest enemy?

Over the next sections, you will learn the answers to these questions. You will learn a lot about who you really are and why you are like you are, how you became that way and what you can do to be the way you want to be.

It is crucial to your overall success to begin with a strong foundation to support the productive behaviors, the appropriate competencies and disciplines within the "Buyer Focused" Velocity Selling System.

As you may have already determined, YOU are the most important person in the world and you are at the center of the target—the core or the bull's-eye. Your attitude toward yourself is the core. Focus on the core of the target and you will hit the bull's-eye more often. But to do that you need to know yourself.

One of the best ways to get to know yourself is to read and do the exercises in my previous book *Disciplined for Life, You are the Author of Your Future.* (see Bibliography). There are twelve disciplines in the book but for now let's focus on Discipline #1, Know Your Rights.

There are ten rights included under Discipline #1, but I want to reinforce only four that are particularly important for salespeople.

Know Your Rights

You have the right to like yourself as you are.

> *Nothing splendid has ever been achieved except by those who dared believe that something inside of them was superior to circumstances.*
>
> **—Bruce Barton**

I believe that we all came into this world as miracles, and as equal human beings regardless of race, religion, color, nationality, sex, title or role.

However, from the day you were born, you have been exposed to many external influences—family, religion, education, friends, politics, the media, and so on. Without you realizing it, many of these external influences have entered your mind and affected the way you are today.

While some of those influences and experiences are positive, many are negative. It is these influences and experiences that have created the beliefs, fears and limitations generating the negative messages, or baggage, that we all carry and must deal with.

Most of us go through life accepting too many external comments that lead us to believe we are not good enough, attractive enough, strong enough, experienced enough, and the list goes on. Until we realize who we really are, from the inside out, we can fall into these traps and stay there.

In our younger years, we picked up a lot of baggage. Some of it was good and some of it was not so good. Most of the time, as children, we believed what we were told. Many people received positive reinforcement. Others received negative comments. Anyone who was overweight, underweight, tall or short, handicapped or different knows what I am talking about. The comments that we accepted as truth became part of us and led us to liking ourselves, or disliking ourselves, as we are.

As we grew older, we also compared ourselves to others and wished we had their looks, size, shape or qualities. On many occasions, we may not have liked ourselves as we are, mostly because of external influences or comments. On other occasions, in certain environments, we liked ourselves as we are, either because of internal beliefs or external influences and comments.

Therefore, in moving forward, it is important for you to understand BAFAR—your beliefs determine your attitudes, your attitudes determine how you feel. How you feel determines the actions you take and your actions determine the results you get in life.

If you want to change your results in life, you have to take action. But to take action, you have to change the way you feel. The way you feel is determined by your attitude, but your attitude is created from your beliefs. What do you believe about you? If you don't believe in you, will anyone else believe in you?

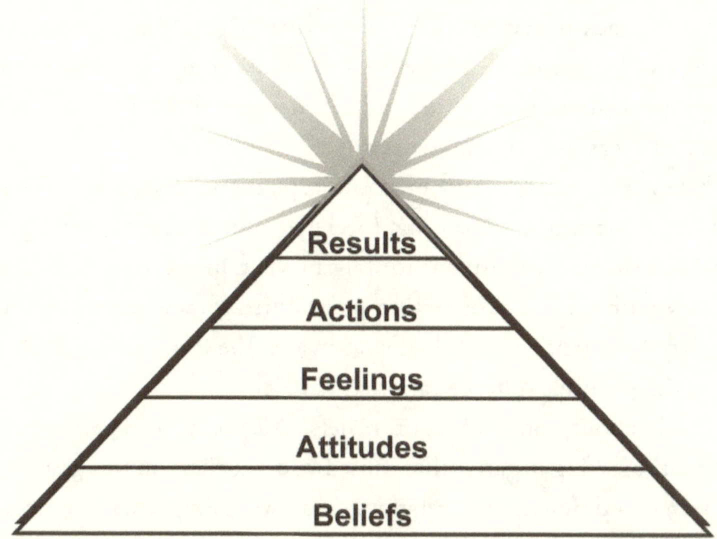

Allow me to share an example on how the BAFAR system works, based on what audiences all over the world have told me they believe about rainy days.

When I ask participants what they believe about rainy days, I naturally get a variety of responses. However, most people in rainy parts of the world believe that rainy days are gloomy days.

So, if you believe rainy days are gloomy, what do you think your attitude would be like? The responses I get are: depressed, negative, sad and so on.

If that were your attitude, how would you feel? The responses I get are: lazy, achy, tired and so on.

If you feel that way, what actions do you take? The responses I get are: take no action, stay in bed, sleep and so on.

If you take those actions, what results do you think you will get? The responses I get are none! However, I like to jokingly say, nine months later you may get a surprise.

Like many of these participants, I believed the same about rainy days; but I have since changed my beliefs. Allow me to share a story with you on how I did it.

While vacationing at a cottage, I was watching raindrops fall into the lake. After half an hour or so my wife suggested I pick up a book and read. However, I decided to go for a walk in the rain instead. I got soaked!

When I came in, I quickly dried myself off, turn on my laptop and started writing my book *Disciplined for Life, You Are the Author of Your Future.* I could not stop writing, but as the rain stopped, I stopped.

Later I went back to review what I had written. I could not believe what I was reading; it was so inspirational. So I started to question myself, using the rule of 3+ which we will learn about later. In the end, I concluded that raindrops were drops of inspiration, and I was only the messenger.

I now believe that rainy days are my most inspirational days, and I walk in the rain whenever I can. My attitude is inspiring, I feel great, I take actions, and I get results.

In 2006, I made a commitment to walk in the rain every time it rained and to write an article with the desire of getting it published somewhere in the world. That year, I got sixty-four articles published worldwide. The funny thing is, that number is how many times I walked in the rain that year.

Now think about some of your beliefs. Maybe you experienced, or were influenced by, something negative that caused you to believe in things as you do. You may have been of a different race, religion, color, wore eyeglasses or braces, were tall or short, fat or skinny, or whatever. You allowed those external comments to enter your mind, and with added emotions, you sent a strong message to the subconscious mind, which in turn worked with the laws of nature to make it a reality. It became part of your belief system.

As an adult, you should be able to distinguish between fact and fiction, what is real and what is not. It is time to revisit your beliefs and change them if you wish. Only you can change your beliefs, and as you do, your attitude, the way you feel, the actions you take and the results you get will also change.

For example, as a young boy, my mother, aunts and grandmother would always grab my cheek and tell me how cute and special I was because I had dimples. When I started going to school, the girls told me I was cute. By the time I was ten, I believed I was cute.

All of that positive feedback built my self-esteem and gave me confidence and self-respect. It made me feel good about myself.

By the time I became a teenager, life took a turn on me—the law of opposites. Those cute dimples turned into ugly pimples. What do you think society told me then? Right, I was ugly. And the more times I would look into the mirror, the more I agreed with them. I was ugly. I became extremely shy. I avoided people and going out, basically losing five years of my life in the process.

Finally, someone approached me and told me about a girl who wanted to go to the graduation dance with me. It took me three weeks and a lot of courage to ask her. Shortly afterwards, my wife-to-be looked beyond what she saw on the outside because the acne didn't matter to her. She gave me the gift of inner strength.

It was that newly found inner strength that caused me to wake up one day and look into the mirror again. As I looked into the mirror, I came to a great realization. Everyone has an outer shelter—skin—that they can hide behind. It is what is behind that skin that really matters. Yes, I had acne, but I came to the conclusion that I liked the guy inside. As I realized this, I started to emerge from my shell. From that point on, I decided to take control of my life and lead my life from the inside out, as opposed to the outside in. In fact, it was this inside-out approach that gave me the courage to eventually become a professional speaker and sales trainer.

Since then, I've liked myself as I am. I know myself, my values, my strengths and weaknesses, my dreams and desires.

Now let's take a look at this same process as it affects the role of a salesperson. Society could have influenced you to believe that the worst job in the world is to be a salesperson. Think about this for a moment. You are part of the general public and not a salesperson. I want you to tell me what comes to mind when you hear the word "salesperson."

This is a valuable exercise in our training sessions. You see, most of us are raised to believe that we should become a professional of sorts. Until recently, Sales was never considered as a serious profession. When asked this question, even professional salespeople, acting as members of the general public, will use such words as "sleazy," "cheat," "money hungry," "Herb Tarlic," "used car salesman," "plaid suits," "sneaky," "liars," and so on, to describe salespeople.

Is that the image you want to portray? No. So what do you do? You hide behind other fancy titles like "account manager," "business development manager," or "product specialist." Why, because you don't like being referred to as a salesperson. Yet, are you any different? No. You keep doing what all other salespeople have done and eventually you will be perceived just as they are. Later in the C: Competency category, I will show you how doing the opposite of traditional sales techniques will make you different and gain you a great deal of respect. So much respect that you will be proud to call yourself a salesperson.

As a certified sales professional I am very proud of my profession. Are you? If so, when putting your children to bed, you would have no problem telling them why they should grow up like you and be a professional salesperson. Very few of us can do that because of the general public perception of salespeople. How can you put your child to bed saying, "I want you to grow to be a sleazy, money-hungry, used car salesperson?" Instead, we raise them to be doctors, lawyers and engineers. These professions are no different than ours. Each of them, like sales, requires the attitude, behavior and competencies of that profession. The main difference between these professions and the sales profession is the amount of respect salespeople have for their buyer's time. Rarely does a sales professional have their buyer wait on them. If you don't like yourself as a salesperson, or as you are, consider doing or being something different. As a salesperson, you have to have a passion for sales, a desire to solve other people's problems. But, how can you solve their problems when you can't solve your own problems? You have to like yourself as you are, to believe in yourself, before anyone else will.

You have the right to fail.

Failure is the opportunity to begin again more intelligently.

—Henry Ford

When society realizes the good that comes out of failure, and recognizes people for trying, the world will be better for it. All success comes from failure. No one in the world has succeeded without first trying, failing, learning, making changes, and moving on. Always remember that you have the right to fail; you no longer have to make excuses for your failed attempts. Instead, reflect on that failure and learn from it. That experience will provide you with better judgment for the future, and will eventually lead you to success.

Success is based on good judgment. Good judgment comes from experience. And how does one get experience? Sometimes we have to fail often to succeed once. But that fear of failure stops us from even trying. And that is one of the reasons we procrastinate. We think about it too much; we hesitate. If you just do it and fail, what is the worst thing that can happen? You will learn a lesson. If you really want to succeed, you may have to double your failure rate. Isn't this what sales is all about?

After losing five of my teenage years hiding with acne, I realized I had some catching up to do. I developed a "do-it-now" attitude. I no longer thought endlessly about things because I realized that the longer I thought about doing something, the longer I would hesitate before doing it; or, I might not do it at all. I put procrastination behind me and started to just do things without thinking, realizing that the worst that could happen is that I would learn something.

Failure is part of my daily life. I don't always take the time to think things out. I am a doer. I learn and move forward by doing. This approach gives me lots of opportunities to fail, and to be criticized. I have experienced so much failure in my life that I am now wise because of it. I learn from every experience. I really see failure as a learning opportunity.

Are you giving yourself sufficient learning opportunities?

I believe that both failure and success are part of life's balance. The more you try, the more you fail, and the more you succeed. If you don't try, you'll neither fail nor succeed.

If you fear failure, you will almost certainly fail. Because of fear, many of us don't take action. We procrastinate. Fear paralyzes the faculty of reason, destroys the faculty of imagination, kills self-reliance, undermines enthusiasm, discourages initiative, leads to uncertainty of purpose, encourages procrastination, and weakens self-control. Fear removes the charm from a personality, destroys ambition, clouds memory and invites failure. It leads to sleeplessness, misery and unhappiness.

Fear is nothing more than a state of mind, and everyone has the ability to control his or her own state of mind. Do you think your fears are the same as everyone else's? Do you think they are justified by the real world? Are your fears my fears? Your fears are your fears and no one else's! Your fears exist only in your mind. Only you can overcome those fears.

The three biggest obstacles in life are indecision, doubt and fear. Indecision is the seed of fear. Indecision grows into doubt and together the two become fear. We fear so many things, from failure to death. Some fears are justified. But other unnecessary fears can take root and grow unless you get rid of the indecision and doubt that grow into fear.

But before you can master fear, you must know its name, habits and origin. When I was in my early twenties, I was afraid to try public speaking. I was concerned that my language and my appearance were not good enough to stand in front of a crowd and speak. I dreaded rejection and criticism as a result of being criticized as a teenager by my friends. This fear prevented me from doing something I really wanted to do—to earn more by speaking to large groups.

Then, with some coaching, I developed enough self-confidence to finally give it a try. And the audience applauded! My fear could have set me back forever. Instead, I got on stage again the next day and spoke in front of another group of people. I faced my biggest fear head-on and I got my first standing ovation! That was enough to give me the confidence to keep going, and to accomplish my dream of becoming a professional speaker and a mass-volume salesperson.

It all starts with courage. Courage is about taking action. It requires discipline, vitality and guts to face the tasks that make you feel uncomfortable. For example, accepting a "no" in sales isn't an act of courage, unless a "no" bothers you. Courage belongs to every salesperson that faces an inner fear. It is deciding to deal with your fear that takes courage.

What a shame that we are sometimes so overwhelmed by our fears that we can't see our finest characteristic is about to take us to new heights… and its name is courage.

Here are some short quotations I review when I need courage to face fear. You may want to refer to these quotes when you are held back because of fear.

Do the thing you fear most and you will control fear.

—Bobby Charleton

Do the thing you fear to do and keep doing it; that is the quickest and surest way ever discovered to conquer fear.

—Dale Carnegie

We have nothing to fear but fear itself.

—Franklin D. Roosevelt

Courage is not the absence of fear, but rather the judgment that something is more important than fear.

—Ambrose Redbone

It is the mind that maketh good of ill, that maketh wretch or happy, rich or poor.

—Edmund Spenser

Worry is a state of mind based upon fear. It paralyzes one's reasoning faculty, destroys self-confidence and initiative.

—Napoleon Hill

Failure will never overtake you if your determination to succeed is strong enough.

—Og Mandino

I would rather be a failure in something that I love than a success in something that I didn't.

—George Burns

Our greatest glory is not in never failing, but in rising every time we fall.

—Confucius

Develop success from failures. Discouragement and failure are two of the secret stepping stones to success.

—Dale Carnegie

In summary, one of the things we fear most is failure. You must realize, though, that you learn from failure. You can overcome the fear of failure by giving yourself permission to fail. Keep in mind that success is based on good judgment and good judgment is based on experience. And how does one get experience? Right—through trial and failure.

Failure is not easy to accept, but there is another way to get around it. When people fail, they have a tendency to beat themselves up through their self-talk. When you do this, you are lowering your self-confidence, your self-esteem, your self-respect and your self-worth. You do this to the point where you no longer take risks or try to do something out of the ordinary. You have become like many other people who have stopped taking risks.

The alternative is to rebuild that courage you used to have as a child—to do things and to accept failure as a part of life's learning.

However, when you fail, do not beat yourself up—look for the lesson learned. Once you have found a lesson learned, build yourself up and pat yourself on the back for having the courage to do something you have not done before. This behavior in turn will build your self-confidence, your self-esteem, your self-respect and your self-worth. It will give you the courage to succeed in life and make you feel good about yourself.

Warning: Patting yourself too often on the back can get to your head. To avoid ego trips, always end the pat on the back with a hand movement across the neck, indicating that you do not want it to get to your head.

You need to be able to see the good behind every experience in life. Rather than criticizing yourself or others for failure, recognize the things that were done right, the effort of trying, and the lessons learned.

So, what is stopping you from moving forward?

The first and best victory is to conquer self. To be conquered by self is, of all things, the most shameful and vile.

—Plato

You have the right to ask.

> *Ask and it shall be given you; seek and ye shall find; knock and it shall be opened unto you. For every one that asketh receiveth; and he that seeketh, findeth; and to him that knocketh it shall be opened.*
>
> **—Luke 11:9-10**

As I speak to audiences around the world, I always ask, "Why don't people ask for what they want?" The answers I get are: "fear of rejection," "fear of losing face" or "being embarrassed." All of them relate to fear of what *may* happen. We will discuss fear in detail in a later chapter titled "Know Yourself," but for now let's understand a few things about asking.

If you don't ask, you don't get. Right?

By simply not asking, the answer is automatically a "NO"! In my mind, that simple act of not asking causes you to automatically lose. Why? Because if you had the courage to ask, you would increase the odds of getting a yes. Are the odds not 50/50?

Just the simple act of asking increases your odds of getting a positive response. And if you got a NO, did you lose anything? No! How can you lose something you never had?

Therefore, make it a habit to ask, but be careful what you ask for, because you may just get it!

Imagine the salesperson who doesn't ask questions to understand the buyer's needs or ask for the order. Picture the person who doesn't ask for the promotion, the person who doesn't ask for a hand in marriage. Do they get what they want?

Don't ever be too shy to ask. What is the worst response you can get? "No." So, what have you lost? You can't lose something you never had. Now, imagine you ask the same question and the answer is yes, just for asking. How much further ahead would you be now?

If I hadn't asked my wife, Joan, to go to the high school graduation with me, I may never have found that wonderful and loving partner. If I hadn't asked my friend John for a thirty-day loan, we might not have been able to build our first home or live in our dream home of today. If I hadn't asked for guidance, I likely wouldn't have received it. And if I hadn't asked myself what I wanted out of life, I doubt I'd be where I (happily) am today.

ASK is a short form for a very important message, one that has been around for over two thousand years and is most accurate.

A stands for Ask, and when you ask you will receive. S stands for Seek, and when you seek, you will find. K is for Knock, and when you knock, the door will be opened. First ask yourself what you want out of life. Once you know what you want, you can go seeking. It is in the seeking that the doors of opportunity will come your way. All you have to do then is have the courage to knock, or ask.

Ask of yourself, ask of others, and ask often. Don't ever be shy to ask. If you don't ask, you don't get. Indeed, the more you ask, the more you get. If you need help, if you want a promotion, if you want a referral, if you do not understand something, if you want more out of life, what must you do?

Ask! You do have the right to ask! Make it a habit to ask.

Later in Category C, Competencies Part 1, you will gain a better appreciation of asking questions and what asking questions can do for you and your success as a salesperson. For now, just get over the fear of asking. We will deal with the fear of rejection shortly.

You have the right to decide how you will use your time and energy.

> *The whole secret of freedom from anxiety over not having enough time lies not in working more hours, but in the proper planning of the hours.*
>
> **—Frank Bettger**

You have a sales job and other responsibilities where there are expectations of you. But who decided to take on these responsibilities? I understand; you needed a job and you had no choice. I've been there. But think about this: is what you are doing bringing you closer to the realization of your success? If so, great! If not, maybe you should reconsider how you are using your time and energy. You have the right to decide how much effort you invest toward achieving your goals. (In Category B, we will discuss time management for sales professionals in greater detail.)

I once worked for a large corporation that had a performance review process. Employees and their supervisors set objectives for the year and reviewed them quarterly. Individuals spent a lot of time and energy on the reviews and appraisals—up to five days a year. This was a great form of discipline and worth the effort because feedback improves job performance.

But whose performance is being appraised? Is that appraisal, or feedback, an internal or an external process?

By the way, who is the most important person in the world? How much time and energy do we provide directly to *that* person and his or her success?

Similarly, as salespeople you claim to spend your time qualifying and understanding the needs of buyers. (Qualifying, as it is used in this book, means determining whether the buyer has a need, a want, a budget and the capability of making a decision to purchase your product or service.) But I wonder how many of you have taken the time to qualify yourselves and understand the needs of the person you see in the mirror.

How many jobs will you go through to find career happiness? How much time and energy will you invest to discover your own needs and desires? Have you set out an annual or lifetime plan of action? Are you reviewing your performance on a regular basis? Remember, you have the right to decide how you will use your time and energy.

Understanding and believing in these four rights—the right to like yourself as you are, the right to fail, the right to ask, and the right to decide how you will use your time and energy—will make a significant difference in your sales success.

Who Am I?

Over the years and in many speaking engagements, I have recommended the following exercise to help participants discover their real "identity" as people get hung up in their roles.

We all play a variety of roles in life. Let's start by identifying some of the roles that you play or positions you hold in life, for example, parent, spouse, student, manager, sales professional and so on.

List the many roles that you play.

Rate your role performance in each of the roles you listed on a scale from 1 to 10, 1 being "poor" and 10 being "great."

Under Identity rate yourself on a scale from 1 to 10, 1 being "poor" and 10 being "great" next to each role rating.

List of Roles	Role Rating (1-10)	Identity Rating (1-10)
____________	________	________
____________	________	________
____________	________	________
____________	________	________
____________	________	________
____________	________	________
Average Rating	________	________

Let's review some of your ratings, particularly those ratings that are under 6. There could some good reasons for ratings under 6. One of them could be that you are new at this role and still learning. Another could be that you hate this role and everything surrounding it. In other words, you are not enjoying it, you're demotivated. It could also be an area of weakness.

For ratings above 6, you probably have a lot of experience in this role and have been recognized for your achievements—you enjoy it and are motivated. It could also be an area of strength.

Note that all the numbers you selected for identity are probably the same as or less than the rating you gave for your roles.

Why? Because most of us have been socially driven to succeed in, and strive for, higher role levels. In other words, our roles define who we are, and, in turn, our identity is then strongly associated with our roles, which may not be our true identity.

Let me demonstrate more clearly what I mean.

Let's pretend you rated your job role as a 9. You have been in the job for years and have been recognized for your high performance. How does that make you feel about yourself—your identity? Well, that identity rating could be as high as a 9.

Now, what would happen if you were let go from your job today? You lost your role. That role rating of a 9 would drop to zero. How would that make you feel about yourself——your identity. Probably like a zero.

Think about this for a moment. How many people do you know who have lost their jobs, their role in life? With the loss of their role, they have lost their identity, in some cases their family. Sadly, some individuals in these circumstances have turned to drugs, alcohol and even committed suicide.

Another way of looking at this is to think of those people who are close to retirement and remind us almost daily that they only have three years to go, then two, then one and so on. They finally retire. What happens to them within five years?

If you answered that they die, you are right. At least that is the answer I get from participants all around the world. Is that what retirement is all about—to work hard all of our lives, look forward to retirement and then to die within five years?

There is a better way—doing the opposite of what society has led us to believe. To fully understand this statement, you need to first answer the following question:

Who am I, without roles?

When answering this question, imagine yourself alone, with no roles. Who is this person? Look into the mirror, what do you see? How do you rate this person without roles on a scale of 0 to 10: 0 being a "nobody" and 10 being "someone to watch out for."

In an upcoming chapter, you will have the opportunity to get to know yourself better, but what you need for now is your identity rating.

If your identity rating is below 6, you have low self-confidence, self-esteem and self-respect. You are focused on your weaknesses and not your strengths, as you should be. You are reactive to the world around you and not in control of your life. You have been leading your life from the outside in.

If your identity rating is above six, the opposite holds true. You have a plan of action. You are proactive and making things happen while living your passion and the life of your dreams.

Your identity and how you feel about yourself is most important.

David Sandler said, "*You can perform in your roles only in a manner that is consistent with how we see yourself conceptually.*"

In other words, your role performance corresponds directly to your identity rating, every time. This means if you see yourself as a "3" you will perform in your roles as a "3." But, if you see yourself as a "10" you will perform as a "10." It all starts from the inside and how you see or feel about yourself.

Your level of identity reflects your level of self-esteem, self-confidence, self-respect, and so on. When you add it all up, it equals your self-worth. Your self-worth equals your net worth!

What value do you place upon yourself? What is your net worth?

You came into this world as a miracle, a high 10. You have been exposed to the external world and have internalized its messages. You have tried things, failed and may have verbally beaten yourself up. You have created your own fears and limitations. You have accepted criticism and have criticized yourself, and in turn, have devalued yourself from a 10 to your present rating.

You may have lost your childhood courage, self-esteem, self-respect and self-confidence. You may no longer value yourself as a 10.

If that is the case, go back to your beliefs. You are an adult now and can distinguish between fact and fiction, what is real and what is not. It is time to change your beliefs about yourself and get yourself back to a 10. Only you can do that for you.

Self-esteem and self-confidence will give you the courage and discipline to do the things you always wanted to do. Lack of self-confidence or self-esteem will cause you to procrastinate, not make decisions, take little or no risk, and leave life to chance.

When you focus on your internal identity, you will experience the greatest of miracles. After all, who is the most important person in the world?

Let's now take a look at why so many people have a fear of cold calling. Is it because of an increased chance of rejection? Of course it is. No one likes to be rejected, but if you know how to deal with rejection, it is not a problem. First answer this question for yourself: when you are rejected is it the role or the identity that is being rejected? If you answered "the role," you are right. The problem arises when we allow role rejection to enter into identity rejection—when we start to take things personally.

That statement reminds me of the circumstances many years ago when I went through several interviews for a sales position with IBM. Each interview was great, except they tried something on the final interview that got me. All along I was asking the right questions and giving the right answers. Then in the final interview they told me they had made a decision not to hire me. I was rejected and I took it personally, instead of challenging it. Later, I learned that it was part of their selection process to see how the interviewees dealt with rejection and how we could turn it around into a sale. I failed, but I did learn a valuable lesson.

Imagine how much more productive you would be if you didn't allow fear and rejection to step in your way. The funny thing is, both are a state of mind and we can control our states of mind. Let's take a look at the following diagram to understand how the mind and body work in unison.

Sales Success Programming

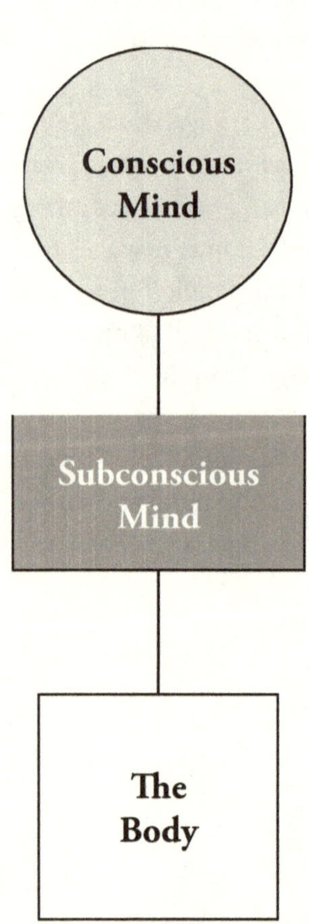

Conscious Mind

- Where ideas are formatted
- Where information is generated through five senses
- Free will resides here
- Pain, pleasure and limitation originate here
- Has ability to accept or reject
- Has ability to dream
- Has ability to concentrate

Subconscious Mind

- The Storage Center
- No ability to reject
- Must accept every thought your conscious mind chooses to accept
- Will create whatever is necessary to fulfill every idea the conscious mind conceives
- Uses all the forces of nature to produce results
- More susceptible to the influence of feelings or emotions

The Body

- An instrument of the mind, mirroring your thoughts and feelings
- Acts out the behavior and actions that govern your result

Make a Decision

This could be a turning point for you. You have the right to decide how you want to live your life. People who have lived full lives haven't done so by accident. They've made a conscious decision sometime during their life that they were going to accomplish something and live the life of their choice.

You, too, can live the life of your choice. You could live the life of someone else's choice, or you may settle for a combination of your desires and those of someone else. You could decide not to make a decision at all. The point is that no one else is going to make that decision for you—you must make it for yourself. Until you make that decision, you will drift aimlessly through life, directed by circumstances and external factors, instead of shaping your own future. Whichever way you decide, make the effort to stick to that choice.

When I realized that my life was my choice, and I was the only one responsible for it, I took full advantage of my decision-making capabilities. I decided to live the life of my choice, of my dreams, to the best of my capability. If you don't make a choice, you are just passing through and leaving life to chance. Don't settle for circumstances or chance. Life is not about chance, it's about choice! You have the freedom to choose the life you want. The first step is to decide that you are going to live the life of your choice.

Do you avoid making decisions? If you said yes, you are not alone. Many people freeze when faced with decisions, even small ones. They are afraid of making the wrong choice. Believing in your own ideas, abilities, and decision-making capabilities is the first step to achieving success in life.

Dr. Wayne W. Dyer said, "*If you're one of those people who hate to make decisions, you can be sure of one thing. This inability to make decisions can stop you dead in your tracks and hinder you on the road to success.*"

You end up waiting for things to happen instead of making them happen.

You doubt your commitments and you turn away from your dreams, the dreams you know could be achieved. The result is tremendous unhappiness, multiple failures and lost opportunities, deep frustration, endless procrastination and abiding hopelessness.

There is something you can do about this. You can gain confidence in your ability to make decisions and make the process easier and more successful. You have a range of options to choose from when you must make a decision. You discard an option when you withdraw yourself from it. An option becomes a decision when you invest yourself in it.

What makes a decision work? It is almost always the decision maker, and not the choice, that makes it work. Failure is proportional to the lack of dedicated commitment. Choices are good only if you make them good.

The first step of a successful decision is to make that decision. The act of making a decision is almost always more important than the substance of the decision itself. Conversely, making no choice—indecision—invalidates all options because it paralyzes us. But the more we make decisions, the more natural the process becomes.

To live the life of your choice you will have to be internally driven. You will need to take an inside-out approach to life. You will need to be consciously aware of what is being said or happening around you and decide if you want to be part of that external environment. If not, you must find or create the environment that is conducive to who you want to be and where you want to go, as we are all products of our environment.

There are three types of people in this world:

1. There are those who are uncertain—they just don't know or can't decide. As teenagers, most of us didn't know what we wanted.
2. There are those who wish and dream, but do nothing about it.
   These are the type of people who depend on a winning lottery ticket. You've heard about them: "If I won a million dollars, I would…" They expect something for nothing and they don't realize there is a price to pay for everything in life—they need to make an effort.
3. There are those who know what they want, plan for it, and go out and get it. They make it happen! These are the people others usually call lucky. But these people had a dream, created a plan, applied it, persisted, and maybe even failed many times along the way, until they got what they wanted.

Which type have you been up to now?

[ ] Type 1 [ ] Type 2 [ ] Type 3

Which type do you want to be from now on?

[ ] Type 1 [ ] Type 2 [ ] Type 3

You just made a decision. If you didn't, go back and make that decision now, as you will soon have to make more decisions.

If you decided you wanted to be a Type 1 or Type 2, nothing will change. You will remain externally driven and a product of your environment. If you decided that you want to be a Type 3, you have taken your first step toward personal leadership. You have decided to take control of your life and soar.

This is an everlasting, internally driven process. This is where true motivation is found. The first step to internal self-motivation is to make decisions—to do something about your life—not just accept what comes along.

Take Control of Your Life

> *You cannot always control circumstances, but you can control your own thoughts.*
>
> —**Charles E. Popplestone**

There are things in life that we cannot control, and things that are under our full control. One of the first things we must do is get into the habit of distinguishing which is which. Then we can start to take control of our lives and our destiny.

Each day we go out into the world where we are faced with the many external influences that are not part of ourselves and not under our control. Influences like the weather, the news, the traffic, the crowds of people or the lack of people, and the comments we hear. When you wake up to a rainy day, rather than a sunny day, do you see things differently? When you get caught in traffic, how do you react? When faced with rejection or failure, what do you do? These things are not under your control, so why do you let them get under your skin?

My philosophy is: *"If you cannot control it, let it be. There is nothing I can do about it."*

However, what is under your control is what is most important.

How you react is under your full control. You have that freedom of choice. You can react as favorably to a rainy day as you would to a sunny day, appreciating what good the rain does, or you can complain about the clouds. When you get caught in traffic you can get upset, which does us no good because you cannot control the traffic, or you can use the time to visualize your dreams. When you face an obstacle you can be discouraged and even quit, or you can seek out the hidden opportunity, knowing that at least you will learn from the experience.

The problem is that most people are not taking control of what is under their control: their thoughts, attitude, self-talk and the way they react to people and circumstances.

The secret is to take control of your thoughts. We all work with one infinite power. We all guide ourselves by exactly the same laws—the natural laws of the universe. The law of attraction, the most powerful law in the universe, states that whatever is going on in your mind, you are attracting to you. The law of attraction says *like attracts like*, so as you think a thought, you are attracting like thoughts to you. Your thoughts of today are your tomorrow.

It doesn't matter who you are or where you are, the law of attraction is forming your entire life experience, and this powerful law is doing that shaping through your thoughts. You are the one who calls the law of attraction into action, and you do it through your thoughts.

A state of mind cannot be purchased, it must be created. Your states of mind are your thoughts. You can improve the quality of your life by managing your thoughts, by reframing them so that they empower rather than depress you. When you focus on thoughts and support them with your self-talk, you not only attract them into your life, you make them part of your belief system. Once they are part of your belief system, you will react accordingly. Take a close look at your beliefs and re-evaluate them.

Your attitude is a direct reflection of your beliefs. Your attitude determines how you feel. It is how you feel that determines how you act. How you act determines your results, all of which are under your control. Are they not?

Let's take a look at your attitude. Do you have an attitude of gratitude? What is your attitude toward yourself? Your attitudes are your thoughts. Do you talk to yourself? What do you say? Is it positive or negative? Are you even aware of what you are saying?

Research says that up to 70 percent of our self-talk is negative and that it takes eleven positive statements to reverse one negative thought. That's a lot of work. Your first challenge is to become aware of what you are saying and what you are thinking, as our thoughts of today dictate the reality of our tomorrow.

How can you control things that are under your control? First, you must become aware of what you are saying or thinking. Then you must decide if this is the way you want it to be. If it is, you accept it and move on. If it is not the way you want it to be, reject it. Put a big solid red X through it. Stop it!

It is only in your conscious state that you can accept or reject an idea or thought. If you use the red X, you will stop that thought from going any further. However, if you do not reject the thought, it moves on to the subconscious mind, which works with the laws of the universe, specifically the law of attraction, to make that thought a reality. The body then reacts according to those thoughts. At this level, it cannot distinguish between positive and negative; it just attracts.

Another method you can use is to place an elastic band on your wrist. Every time you have a negative thought or self-talk, pull the band and let it slap you on the wrist. That will send a message to your conscious mind to reject that thought or message.

Be aware of what you are thinking, saying to yourself or how you react to events that are not under your control. Take the time to eliminate those non-supporting thoughts and remarks, and soon you will be rewarded with the self-control required to be a success in sales. All it takes is twenty-one consecutive days of self-discipline to make it a habit. (See Monthly Monitor Chart in Category B)

What about your habits? Are you controlling your habits, or are they controlling you? Negative habits such as self-criticism, procrastination, indecision and fear lead to failure. Negative thoughts prevent us from accomplishing the things we want in life.

Changing your thought process and habits will require a lot of discipline. Discipline involves doing what you have to do, even when you don't want to do it. It means respecting the commitment you made to yourself and doing whatever it takes to get it done, when it needs to be done. This will be your start to taking control of your life through self-discipline.

Many of my behaviors and habits developed over time. I really learned to master discipline by following the prescribed method of reading *The Greatest Salesman in the World* by Og Mandino. I applied the thirty-day discipline that eventually made me a slave to some good habits and attitudes.

The prescribed method was to read one of ten short scrolls, three times a day for thirty days, before proceeding on to the next scroll. If you missed a morning, noon or evening reading, you had to start that scroll over again from day one. It seemed pretty easy, at first.

A book that could have been read in an afternoon took me eighteen months to complete, as prescribed. But the results astonished me. What do you think would happen to you if you kept repeating the same positive message to yourself three times a day for thirty days?

As an adult, you have absolute control over your own thoughts. Your thoughts control your attitude and determine how you react to situations. Your thoughts are you! You have created your own fears, your own limitations and barriers. You are who you are based on what you have thought about in your past.

I can remember when I was in my twenties working as a sales representative for a major oil company and doing a lot of driving. I drove so much that I could not help but think about the mileage I was doing. I would say to myself that I was increasing my chances of having a car accident because I drove so much. Well, it wasn't long after focusing on that thought that it became a reality, and I totaled a car. Fortunately, no one was injured.

Today, I realize how I created that thought, reinforced it through negative self-talk and invited it to happen. I also realized that my thoughts and self-talk are 100 percent under my control.

The opposite also applies. Many times before going in on a sales call I would take the time to visualize the visit. I would see myself establishing rapport and trust with the buyer and having them like me. I would see myself taking notes and asking qualifying questions and doing a great presentation. I would see the prospect buying and becoming an ongoing friend and client. All this activity was visualized in my mind. I set myself up for success. It was a state of mind.

Because you have the ability to control your own state of mind, you can overcome habits and even fears. You have the capability and the right to accept or reject your thoughts. It's called willpower. If you fail to control your own mind, how can you control anything else? Control your thoughts or your thoughts will control you. There is no halfway compromise. Mind control is a result of self-discipline and habit. Keep your mind busy with a definite purpose backed by a definite plan.

Know Yourself

> *No person has a chance to enjoy permanent success until he begins to look in a mirror for the real cause of all his mistakes.*
>
> **—Napoleon Hill**

In this chapter we are going to have you do some exercises to help you get to know yourself. When you take the time to know yourself, you become internally driven. You need to get to know yourself from the inside out—your values, your motivators and demotivators, your strengths and your weaknesses. Your greatest strength and direction will come from inside you, not from the outside world.

We are easily influenced by people and circumstances, and forget sometimes who we really are and what is important to us. These forces can control us and force us into a mold of conformity, diminishing any thought or action that might develop our individuality and creativity.

If you have no concept of whom or what you are, your journey into the future will be uncertain and dependent upon circumstances—circumstances that are not all under your control. You will wander aimlessly through life. Without a well-defined identity, your ability to succeed will depend on luck. But success is not about luck.

Defining your identity will keep you focused as you set priorities, organize tasks, deal with emergencies and accomplish challenges in your personal and business life.

The first step in defining your identity involves self-awareness—seeing yourself as you really are. It involves being honest with yourself. Taking inventory of yourself can be an uncomfortable and even painful experience, but you must do it in order to move forward.

If you repeatedly hear the words "you can't," it's easy to be convinced that you cannot achieve your dreams. If you hear "anyone who makes a lot of money is a crook," you may be influenced not to make any significant amount of money. On the other hand, a positive message like "anyone who controls their spending can accumulate money" would encourage us to control our spending.

You have the right to select what motivates you and to understand your feelings. The choices you make will direct the course you follow in life.

Over the years, I have had the opportunity to complete a variety of profiling tests. These tests can tell you about your strengths and weaknesses, your personality type and the sorts of work that may suit you. I have learned so much about myself this way that I recommend you take advantage of these opportunities when they arise, to learn about yourself.

I would like you to look inside, or into that mirror in front of you, and complete these exercises before proceeding any further. Sit in a comfortable place, and write down as much as you can. Sleep on it, and then go back and add to your answers. Make any additions or changes that you wish—this is your inventory. There are no wrong answers, but be honest with yourself. The answers are for you only. They will help you better understand yourself—to know who you really are. This is the foundation to the house of success that you are building.

What Are My Values?

Your fundamental beliefs are your values. Values are also known as principles, ideals, convictions or purposes. Your beliefs are important to you, and will motivate you. By clarifying your values, you create a structure upon which you can build your personal and business life. The following exercise will help you set your life's priorities.

The following table lists many of the things that motivate people. Rate each according to how much you value it: always, often, sometimes, seldom or never. Then go back and rank your "Always Valued" checks in order of their importance to you. This exercise should help you determine what matters most to you.

Motivator	Always Valued	Often Valued	Sometimes Valued	Seldom Valued	Never Valued
Advancement					
Adventure					
Aesthetics					
Authority/power					
Challenge					
Change / variety					
Community					
Competence					
Competition					
Creativity					
Decision-making					
Excitement					
Family					
Freedom					
Friendships					
Group affiliations					
Helping others					
Helping society					
Independence					
Influencing people					
Intelligence					
Job security					
Knowledge					
Location of home					
Location of work					
Money					
Moral standards					
New ideas/ things					
Personal contact					

Personal security					
Physical challenge					
Public contact					
Recognition					
Religious beliefs					
Salary level					
Stability					
Status					
Supervision					
Tranquility					
Working alone					
Working under pressure					
Working with people					
Others:					

Now that you have identified your most important values, the ones you always value, go back and rank them in order of priority, as best you can. It is these values that will help you find your passion and motivate you to the realization of your dreams.

Personal Evaluation

This exercise is meant to help you see your situation, understand why you rate yourself as you do, and decide what actions you can take to improve your ratings. It will give you a base to measure your progress as you rate yourself in the future.

Rate yourself from 1 to 10 on how you see or feel about yourself.

1 is poor and 10 is great.

Physical: __________

For example: appearance, medical check-ups, exercise programs, weight control, nutrition

Why did you rate yourself like this?

____

____

____

____

Identify the positive factors

____

____

____

Identify areas for improvement to be a 10

____

____

____

What actions must I take to be a 10?

____

____

____

Family: __________

For example: listening habits, forgiving attitude, good role model, time together, supportive of others, respectful, loving

Why did you rate yourself like this?

____

____

____

Identify the positive factors

____

____

Identify areas for improvement to be a 10

___

___

___

What actions must I take to be a 10?

___

___

___

Financial: ___

For example: earnings, savings and investments, budget, adequate insurance, charge accounts

Why did you rate yourself like this?

___

___

___

Identify the positive factors

___

___

___

Identify areas for improvement to be a 10

___

___

___

What actions must I take to be a 10?

___

___

___

Social: ___

For example: sense of humour, listening habits, self-confidence, manners, caring

Why did you rate yourself like this?

___

___

___

Identify the positive factors

____

____

____

Identify areas for improvement to be a 10

____

____

____

What actions must I take to be a 10?

____

____

____

Spiritual*:* __________

For example: inner peace, sense of purpose, prayer, religious study, belief in God
Why did you rate yourself like this?

____

____

____

Identify the positive factors

____

____

____

Identify areas for improvement to be a 10

____

____

____

What actions must I take to be a 10?

____

____

____

Mental*:* __________

For example: imagination, attitude, continuing education, reading, curiosity
Why did you rate yourself like this?

____

____

Identify the positive factors

____
____
____

Identify areas for improvement to be a 10

____
____
____

What actions must I take to be a 10?

____
____
____

Career*:* ___________

For example: job satisfaction, effectiveness, job training, understanding job purpose, competence

Why did you rate yourself like this?

____
____
____

Identify the positive factors

____
____
____

Identify areas for improvement to be a 10

____
____
____

What actions must I take to be a 10?

____
____
____

List Of Assets And Liabilities

STRENGTHS **I am good at:**	**WEAKNESSES** **I need improvement in:**
1. ____________	1. ____________
2. ____________	2. ____________
3. ____________	3. ____________
4. ____________	4. ____________
5. ____________	5. ____________
6. ____________	6. ____________
7. ____________	7. ____________
8. ____________	8. ____________
9. ____________	9. ____________
10. ____________	10. ____________

Asset Message: Refer to and reread, relish and dwell on these strengths (assets) constantly. They will take you anywhere you want to go, providing you with the energy you need to keep moving forward. Your strengths represent your self-worth.

Liability Message: Pick the top three weaknesses and do something about them. Forget the rest. No one is perfect, nor is that goal realistic.

Understanding My Motivation

Think about an experience in your life that you really enjoyed. Then think about an episode when you had to do something you didn't enjoy. What do those experiences tell you about yourself?

What motivates me?

____

____

____

What demotivates me?

____

____

____

What are some conditioning influences that affect me?

____

____

What are some negative messages that motivate me? (Such as, "You can't do it!")

____

____

____

What are some positive messages that motivate me? (Such as "You can do it!")

____

____

____

FEAR IS NOTHING MORE THAN A STATE OF MIND, and every human being has the ability to completely control his or her own state of mind. Indecision is the seedling of fear. Indecision crystallizes into doubt, and together the two become fear.

The exercise below is intended to help you master your fears. What are your biggest fears?

Fear

What has this fear prevented me from doing?

____

____

____

What experiences caused this fear?

____

____

____

If I face this fear head-on, what is the worst thing that can happen?

____

____

____

What can I do to overcome this fear?

____

____

____

Summary

- You have the right to like yourself as you are, to fail, to ask and to decide how you will use your time and energy.
- Your beliefs determine your attitudes, your attitude determines your feelings, your feelings then determine your actions and your actions determine your results.
- You identified who you are, with and without roles.
- You choose to keep rejection on the role side and recognize the importance of keeping a high identity.
- You followed programming for sales success through the conscious mind to the subconscious and to the body.
- You made a decision, and it is the decision maker who will make that decision work.
- You took control of your attitude, thoughts and self-talk using the Red X, or a rubber band, to control negativity. You also identified your ineffective habits and the effective habits that you want to develop.
- You took the time to know yourself, from the inside out.

ATTITUDE TOWARD YOUR ORGANIZATION

In the last chapter you took the time to get to know the most important person in the world, located at the center of the target. Belief in yourself is a must as no one else will believe in you if you first don't believe in yourself. But there are other components that you also have to believe in when you are in sales. The next ring on the target is your attitude and your level of belief toward your organization.

You may feel real good about yourself and know that you are the best person for the sales job you hold, but for some reason, you don't fully believe in your organization, product or service or the team you work with. You know as well as I do that your attitude and level of belief will be transparent to the buyer and that a purchase will not take place because of it. In turn, you may externalize and blame the organization for a poor product or service, poor delivery times or service. Yet, who is the real problem here?

Answer the following questions:

As a salesperson, how do you feel about your organization on a scale of:

Poor ____ Great

0 1 2 3 4 5 6 7 8 9 10

Why? ____

As a salesperson, how do you feel about your organization's products and services?

Poor ____ Great

0 1 2 3 4 5 6 7 8 9 10

Why? ____

As a salesperson, how do you feel about your fellow team members?

Poor ____ Great

0 1 2 3 4 5 6 7 8 9 10

Why? ____

Are you a team player? ______________________________

If so, how? ____________________________________

If not, why not? _________________________________

Based on your rating response to the previous questions, you either believe strongly in the organization, its products and services and the team members you represent, or you have some work to do to increase your belief. You know as well as I do that your attitude and level of belief will be transparent to the buyer, as your body speaks louder than words. Your average rating is posted on your forehead and your body is demonstrating that rating accordingly.

If your average rating is 6 or less, please take my advice, and leave, because you do not believe. If you do not believe in your organization, products, services or the team, you will underperform and that will cause you to be stressed. That stress will lead to illness and nobody wants that to happen to you. You are better to find another job, one in which you believe.

Allow me to share a personal example with you. I was a door-to-door salesman for a home fire alarm system company. This is when home fire alarms first came into being in the mid-1970s. I believed in myself, the organization, its products and the team that I represented. I worked hard and I did well. Within six months, I overheard a conversation where the organization I represented was being sued because the fire alarm system that we sold did not go off during a fire and someone almost died.

I didn't understand then why my sales dropped, but I do understand today. I was still working hard, but my belief in the reliability of the product fell. I found it difficult to sell something in which I no longer believed. I addressed it with the team, but they found me to be negative. Within a short period of time I left the organization and started selling something in which I did believe. Isn't it funny how we succeed when our belief in something is strong?

If your rating is between 7 and 9, you can stay, but you need to discuss the issues that are holding you back, the "why" answers you wrote. You need to get yourself up to a 10. Only then will buyers be attracted to do business with you, because your body and attitude will demonstrate that you believe in you, your organization, products, services and team members. If even one element is not strong, you will lose the sale.

Belief is the key. What if the business you are working in became yours, or if you became self-employed or on a 100 percent commission doing what you are doing? What would you do differently?

By answering this question you are taking on an owner's mentality. Do you have an owner's mentality toward your job and your organization? If you are proactive, you probably do. However, if you are reactive you probably don't, as you are waiting for someone to tell you what to do.

No matter what business you are in or job you do, you should always treat your job as if it were your own business, particularly when it comes to sales. When you are proactive you are in control. Life is always easier when you are one step ahead of management, and/or the buyer. Consider what an owner's mentality can do for you and your organization.

When we talk about belief in an organization, we ask about your organization's mission statement—do you buy into it? Why? Why not? Does your attitude reflect your belief in the mission statement? Does the sales team's attitude reflect their belief in the mission statement? Does the entire organizational team's attitude reflect their belief in the mission statement? Do you feel that the following areas support the organization toward the attainment of the mission statement internally and externally: Training, Communications, Image, Marketing, Networking, Other?

Imagine an organization trying to navigate without everyone rowing in the same direction. Salespeople are the front line in most organizations. Salespeople usually know the most about the organization they represent and their products and services. They also know the most about the organization's buyers and potential buyers. Salespeople who are not fully comfortable with whom and what they are representing can do more harm than good.

Summary

- Reflect, confirm and take hold of your attitude toward your organization, its products and services and fellow team members
- Develop an owner's mentality by taking ownership of your job and treating it like your own business.

ATTITUDE TOWARD YOUR BUYERS

You have taken the time to get to know the most important person in the world and your attitude and level of belief toward yourself and your organization. Now let's review your attitude and level of belief toward your buyers.

In order to be successful in sales we must believe from within all three components of attitude–yourself, your organization and your buyers.

The first question here is, can your buyers support your products and services? If they can, great! But if you don't think the buyers can, guess what? You're right and your results will show it. You are better to give up and find new buyers for your products and services or a new product or service that will fit the buyer's needs.

I used to sell recreational real estate. I was quite successful at it. I believed in me, the organizations I represented and, for a long time, the buyers I was selling to.

However, with a change in government, the buyers also changed. They stopped purchasing real estate because of the fear of what would happen to their investment under the new administration. Real estate values plummeted, as did my commissions and my belief in the buyer market. I hung in far too long. I believed the buyer market would change, but fifteen years later, it hadn't. In the meantime, I have moved on to bigger and better things. Maybe you should, too, if you don't believe there are buyers for your products or services.

The buyer perception of salespeople can be an issue too. How do your buyers perceive salespeople? How does your buyer perceive you? How would you like them to perceive you? What are you doing about it?

For example, do you walk in to see a buyer with your briefcase full of brochures? If so, you will be perceived by the buyer as the "traditional salesperson." It will be all about you, your organization and your products and services. The barriers will go up and the buyer will see you as a waste of time—the most common complaint about salespeople.

However, let's change our approach, our attitude, and switch the focus to the buyer. How would you be perceived if you arrived at the buyer's office with nothing more than a notepad, ready to ask questions, listen and take notes?

Keep in mind that your buyer makes your living. You have to react to their needs and desires. One of the universal needs of buyers is to be understood, and one of their top desires is to be listened to.

In the case of real estate transactions, I was never licensed. There was no need to be, as I was not selling private lots or homes. I was representing major land developers and builders. Real Estate agents did not have a good reputation at the time. They were battling with each other over commissions and it was a dog-eat-dog business. I wanted nothing to do with it, and deliberately stayed away from that end of the business. It was a good thing that I did, too. Most of them went under during the '80s while I survived because of my engaging and buyer-focused approach.

So how are you positioned in your market? Are you getting the respect you deserve or are you "just like the rest of them?" In order to stand out from the crowd, you have to create your own personal marketing program. I am not talking about the marketing program created by your organization. I am talking about a personal marketing program built *by* you *for* you.

One of the greatest opportunities we have in sales is to develop our reputation and build our network. Some of us are even paid to do just that. With or without a sale, each and every day we are building or destroying our reputation and our network. The key is to build that reputation and network through a personal marketing program.

People buy from people, especially people they like. A personal marketing program will separate you from everyone else. You can position yourself as the leader in the field with the most credibility and respect, *if* you are willing to go the extra mile. The extra mile is simply giving more of your expertise in a manner that is valued by your buyers.

Personal marketing plans will be discussed in greater detail in the "Behavior Toward Your Buyers" chapter in Section B. In the meantime, remember that people buy you first. Do you have a win-win attitude? I hope so, because once they buy *you*, they will buy whatever you are representing.

Are you worth buying into?

Now, take the time to define your market: who are your prospects, what do they look like, where are they located, what are their problems, their needs and desires? Describe your ideal prospect—profile them. Describe your ideal buyer—profile them. What are their likes and dislikes? How do you market to them? How do you meet them? How do you start and maintain a relationship?

Your marketing department likely already asked the above questions, but you need to answer them for yourself based on *your* knowledge. You are the product or service now and you need your own marketing program. People buy whatever you have to sell because of who you are. How do you need to position yourself in the marketplace, your territory or your accounts?

We have discussed belief in your market—the buyers, perceptions, positioning, personal marketing plan and your reputation and network. It all sounds good, but you are not the only one in the market. You probably have some competitors.

Know the Competition

Just as you profiled your ideal buyer, you must also know your competition inside out if you want to position yourself for success. On the following pages, you will find a list of items that you should consider when completing a competitive analysis.

There are many ways to obtain the information. You can get it from websites, buyers who have dealt with your competition, or you can just pick up the phone and ask your competition to tell you about themselves. You will be surprised how much you will learn, as salespeople love to share everything they know without first qualifying the enquiry. Try it and see for yourself what I am talking about.

Having a clear understanding of your competitive advantages in your target market is essential. Knowing your strengths and weaknesses and those of your competition, puts you in an advantageous position. Your job would then be to develop your competitive advantage statement, a statement that is unique to your products or services. Keep it short and to the point.

Competitive Analysis

Rate your organization and your main competitors on a scale of **0** being *low* to **10** being *high* in the following areas. After completing this analysis, prioritize in the "Important" column, 12 of these items for immediate attention.

Competitor

	Us	A	B	C	Important
Product/Service Quality	______	______	______	______	______
Product/Service Selection	______	______	______	______	______
Product/Service Depth	______	______	______	______	______
Unique Product/Service	______	______	______	______	______
Availability	______	______	______	______	______
Product/Service Price	______	______	______	______	______
Guarantees/Warrantees	______	______	______	______	______
Packaging	______	______	______	______	______
Unit of Measure (e.g. doz.)	______	______	______	______	______
Name Brands	______	______	______	______	______
Generic Brands	______	______	______	______	______
Sales Force	______	______	______	______	______
Sales Methods	______	______	______	______	______
Advertising	______	______	______	______	______
Promotions	______	______	______	______	______
Methods of Distribution	______	______	______	______	______
Length of Time in Business	______	______	______	______	______
Credit Policies	______	______	______	______	______
Market Position	______	______	______	______	______
Image/Reputation	______	______	______	______	______
Innovativeness	______	______	______	______	______
Special Skills	______	______	______	______	______
Special Knowledge	______	______	______	______	______
Available Capital	______	______	______	______	______
Available Credit	______	______	______	______	______
Credit for Clients	______	______	______	______	______
Financial Control	______	______	______	______	______
Management Expertise	______	______	______	______	______
Systems & Controls	______	______	______	______	______
Strategic Planning	______	______	______	______	______

Parking	______	______	______	______	______
Training	______	______	______	______	______
Research & Development	______	______	______	______	______
Network/Contacts	______	______	______	______	______
Quality of People	______	______	______	______	______
Visual Merchandising	______	______	______	______	______
Location	______	______	______	______	______
Other	______	______	______	______	______
	______	______	______	______	______
	______	______	______	______	______

Note your differences and use them to your advantage.

What is your unique competitive advantage statement?

____

Summary

- Reflect, confirm and take hold of your attitude toward the market and its buyers.
- Identify the "who, what, where and how's" of your buyer.
- Profile your ideal buyer.
- Develop a win-win attitude.
- Consider a personal marketing plan to position yourself as the expert to the buyers in your market.
- Gain a better understanding of your competition.
- Congratulations, you have now completed Attitude: Belief from Within, the first and most important step of the "Buyer Focused" Velocity Selling System.

Review and Daily Disciplines for Attitude: Belief from Within

In the category of Attitude: Belief from Within, we covered three chapters. You learned four rights and you now have an understanding of the BAFAR system. You understand the importance of accepting failure as a lesson learned and how to build yourself up, versus destroying your self-worth after failing. You also learned to ask and if you don't ask, you don't get. You learned how to decide on more effective use of your time and energy.

You learned "who am I" and "who am I without roles" while discovering the importance of your internal identity and self-worth. You made some decisions about your life, how to take control of it and how to be in control of your thoughts. You completed many exercises and you got to know yourself, from the inside out.

We then looked at attitude toward your organization and your level of belief toward the organization, its products and/or services and the team. You made some decisions either to leave or to get yourself up to a 10, take full responsibility for your job and develop an owner's mentality.

Finally, we learned the importance of your attitude toward your buyers, how your buyers perceive salespeople and how you wanted to be perceived. You learned how to do things differently so that you always add value to the buyer while positioning yourself as an expert in the marketplace with a win-win attitude.

You have almost completed the "Attitude: Belief from Within" section. All that is left for you to do is to reflect on all of the learning you received. It is now time to write out the daily disciplines you want to instil in your life and then do what you have to do. Remember that any behaviors that get recognized or rewarded get repeated, so include them as well.

Daily Disciplines: Attitude: Belief from Within

What did you learn?

____

____

____

____

It is now time to set those ***daily disciplines and do what you have to do.*** Remember that any behavior that gets recognized or rewarded gets repeated.

1. *What daily disciplines do you want to apply for yourself?*

____

____

____

What will your reward be for doing what you say you will do?

____

2. *What daily disciplines do you want to apply toward your Organization?*

____

____

What will your reward be for doing what you say you will do?

____

3. What daily disciplines do you want to apply toward buyers?

____

____

____

What will your reward be for doing what you say you will do?

____

Reminder: review these disciplines daily for the next twenty-one consecutive days, or using the Monthly Monitor Chart for twenty-five out of thirty-one days and you will make these disciplines effective habits.

BEHAVIOR: YOUR BOTTOM LINE

Behavior Toward Yourself

1. Behavior Toward Yourself
2. Why Set Goals, What Is in It for YOU?
3. Know What You Want
4. Group, Categorize, Prioritize
5. Are You Willing to Pay the Price?
6. SMART Goals
7. Creating a Goal Log
   - A. Setting SMART Goals
   - B. Date for Completion
   - C. Outcomes
   - D. Obstacles/Contingencies
   - E. Skills and Behaviors
   - F. People Groups or Resources
   - G. Action Plan
   - H. Methods of Monitoring and Measuring
   - I. Rewards
   - J. Commitment
8. Taking Action
9. Monitoring and Measuring Your Progress

Behavior Toward Your Organization

1. Organizational Goals
2. Call-to-Close Ratios and Tracking Behaviors
3. Pay Time/No-Pay Time

Behavior Toward Your Buyers

1. The ABCs of Targeting
2. Retain and Regain Strategies
3. Gain Strategies
4. Attracting Buyers—Personal Marketing Plan

Behavior: Your Bottom Line

In this category we are going to discuss behavior. Behavior is the manner in which you conduct yourself, the way you act, function or react. The three chapters that follow relate to the goals and behaviors effective at a personal, organizational, and buyer- and market-targeting level. Without goals there is no reason to act, no motivation to take daily actions or go the extra mile.

Appropriate behavior drives opportunities as you will learn to target your sales efforts. Opportunities come from setting goals, written SMART goals. What do you want out of life or out of your business? Who could determine this for you and who can make it happen? What are the daily behaviors that you must apply to live the life of your dreams?

When they are applied, it is those daily behaviors, and learning that will make a big difference in your level of sales success. For example, as salespeople we need to constantly network; call on and qualify prospects; present to them and help them buy; and follow up. When is the best time to conduct these behaviors? Once you identify these behaviors and times and stick to them, watch your time management skills and results improve dramatically.

Now let's take a look at your market. Do you know where the bulk of your business is coming from? Can you clearly define the buyers? Do you have a good handle on whom you should be targeting in on—that is, if you want a maximum return on your investment in time? Then as you target in, are you in a position to obtain pertinent industry, organizational and buyer information?

All of these behaviors will be discussed in the following pages. But before we proceed, let's go back to the center of the target—you.

BEHAVIOR TOWARD YOURSELF

Behavior, like attitude, starts with you.

Answer this question for me: Why do you go to work?

When I ask participants around the world why they go to work, most of them reply, "to earn a living" or "to make money." When I question them further, using the rule of 3+ technique, which you will learn about in competencies, I find out their true motivation, and it has nothing to do with money.

Most of us go to work to satisfy a personal need, desire or dream that we want to eventually fulfill. Work is only a stepping stone to help us get what we want out of life. It is part of the price we pay to live a dream.

Why do *you* go to work? What is your underlying reason?

Let's first realize that the reason we go to work is different for each of us. The main reason we go to work is to realize one of our dreams or desires.

Once you know your motivation for going to work, you will be more motivated to go, and you will do a better job while you are there. Consider your job or business and what you are doing as a stepping stone to where you want to go, what you want to be or what you want to have. All of these relate to your dreams and desires.

What you do for a living is a choice you've made. But there is a reason you've made that choice and that choice goes beyond making money. Sure, money has something to do with it, but it is not the money that gets you out of bed in the morning—it is what you want to do with the money that keeps you motivated. It is the realization of your dreams, and dreams can be realized when you take the time to organize, plan and put your plan into action.

One of the greatest learning's experiences I have had working in sales was realizing how we were always setting sales targets and objectives, and being measured against them. This is a good practice that keeps us focused on our sales targets. So why not apply those same goal-setting and monitoring strategies to our personal lives so that we too can stay focused on our dreams and end up where we want to be.

In most organizations today, management devotes enormous energy to setting work objectives and conducting performance reviews for individual employees. Corporations go through this time-consuming and costly exercise to ensure the most favorable results for their firm.

In professions such as ours (sales), we spend considerable time questioning, listening, discovering and understanding the needs of buyers in order to provide a recommended solution or action plan.

In contrast, how much time and energy do you expend discovering your own needs and desires, and then consciously setting objectives, developing action plans with measurable performance standards, and finally, reviewing your own performance?

By engaging in such an exercise, you will be doing something about your life. You will be going to work *on* yourself, *for* yourself. This is where the real changes in behavior have to start. Remember the previous question I asked of you—who is the most important person in the world?

In the following sections on behavior toward yourself, we will help you to discover your dreams and organize them into a sense of priority. We will help you to determine if you are prepared to pay the price to make those dreams a reality. You will learn how to set goals and create a goal logbook.

The process, once you learn how to use it for yourself, is the same for setting your sales and organizational goals. If you want to be a success in your organization, you first have to demonstrate successful behaviors to yourself, as you cannot give something of value to someone else if you do not have it inside to give away. I want you to learn how to set SMART goals and demonstrate appropriate behaviors toward yourself first, so you in turn can give those successful behaviors to your organization or business.

Earl Nightingale said, "Success is the progressive realization of worthwhile goals."

Are you ready to commit yourself to developing personal and organizational goals, making plans and taking action accordingly?

When you believe in your dreams, nothing but self-imposed limitations will stop you from achieving them. Your first step is to define your dreams as goals. A goal is a specific and measurable result that must be achieved within a specified time, and resource and cost constraints. A goal is an end, a result, and not just a task to be performed. It describes the condition we want to achieve. Our goals guide our actions and help us plan at work and at home. When we focus on our goals, long- and short-range, our present is determined by our future ... not our past.

Visualize your first goal. Clearly understand your destination. Now the steps you take will all be in the right direction. You can examine each part of your life in the context of what really matters to you. Your goals are an extension of your values.

Goal setting is the process you use to select, define and put into operation the expectations you have for yourself.

Why Set Goals? What's in It for You?

Goal setting focuses your efforts and improves your direction in life.

Goal setting causes you to set priorities and become more organized.

Goal setting turns your wishful thinking into reality.

Goal setting points out to you your successes as you achieve them, motivating you on to further success.

Goal setting can improve your self-esteem.

Goal setting makes you responsible for your own life. It causes you to define your own value system.

Goal setting makes you aware of your strengths, which you can use to overcome obstacles and solve problems.

Goal setting points out your weaknesses. You can begin setting new goals to improve in those areas and turn them into strengths.

Record keeping is important. Writing down your goals and action plans represents a commitment. Otherwise, your dreams are merely wishful thinking. You can reread and visualize written goals. They are credible and legitimate. They live and lead you onward. When you write you have begun to act. Inertia is gone. You sense accomplishment already.

Know What You Want

You have the right to your dreams, desires and expectations.

This chapter is dedicated to identifying, and writing down, all of your dreams, desires and expectations that you would like to realize in your life, as you must know what you want out of life in order to get it. Without knowing what you want, you will go through life aimlessly, like a ship without a rudder. Until your dreams are written down, they will merely be wishes.

When I was twenty-two years old, I took a sick day from work, as I was truly sick at how my life was going nowhere. I sat down at the dining room table and asked myself a very important question, what do I want out of life?

As I sat there thinking, I picked up a pencil and pretended it was a magic wand—there were no limitations or barriers and anything I wrote down would become a reality. I started writing down my thoughts on a pad of paper, and gave myself twenty-four hours to complete the exercise. I wrote down every thought that came to mind, no matter how ridiculous, or impossible, it might have been. I just kept writing and writing. I even woke up in my sleep and added a few more thoughts.

The next morning, just before I got to work, I completed a list of all my desires in life. Within twenty-four hours, I had filled the whole pad of paper with all of my thoughts, dreams and life desires. I no longer felt ill. I felt great, saying this is all I wanted out of life. I felt a sense of direction.

I reviewed that list and had it handy for the following six months, until I lost it. Eighteen years later, I found the list as we were moving from our first dream home to our second. As I reviewed that list, what do you think was going through my mind?

It was incredible how many of the things that I had written down had become a reality and how those that hadn't were still on my list. The secret is that a dream will remain a dream until you write it down. Once it is written down, it crystallizes the dream and increases its chances of becoming a reality. You too can experience that same sensation by completing the following exercises in your workbook. These exercises will become the basis for the rest of your life.

Start with completing your List of Dreams. Set a timeframe in which you will write down all of your dreams, desires and expectations of life. I gave myself twenty-four hours—a day of my life that made the biggest difference in my life.

Find a comfortable place where you will not be disturbed. You may want to play some inspirational or relaxing music to help you along. Have some extra paper and pencils with you, or just create a file on your computer where you can list all of your dreams.

List your dreams—write down every possible and crazy dream that comes to mind. In order for this exercise to be effective you must accept that nothing is impossible. There are no barriers, obstacles or excuses why something can't happen.

The objective is to write down every thought or desire that comes to your mind, no matter how silly, impossible or crazy it is.

This is not a test. There are no wrong answers. Write down everything you'd love to have, do or be.

Write down whatever your heart desires. Just keep writing. Everything is possible. Invest time in yourself and write every thought that comes into your mind within your allocated time frame. Pretend that if it is not written down, it will never happen. Sleep on it and write any thoughts that come to mind during the night. Wake up and do the same, and then stop and say, "This is all that I want out of life."

This is just the beginning, but if you do not write it down, it is guaranteed not to happen. Invest in yourself, make the time and have fun!

Your objective is to write all of your dreams and desires for the next six months; for the next year; five years; and for life. Write, write, write and keep writing. Identify everything you want to have, be or do at some point in your life. Remember, there are no wrong answers and this list is for your reference only. It doesn't have to be neat or organized in any way. Just write every thought that comes to mind. Sleep on it and add more the next day if you like. Keep in mind that there are no barriers and that nothing is impossible. Go ahead and start your list of dreams!

Examples of Dreams

These suggestions might help you write your list of dreams:

Travel and vacations (where and how)
Children and family (education, activities, shared time)
Automobile (kind, color, options)
Friendship (respect, helping others)
House (size, style, extras)
Health (body weight, exercise)
Money (savings, net worth, investments)
Mind (self-esteem, knowledge)
Career (salary increase, promotions, new job, own business)
Education (personal development)
Environment
Sports
Relationships
Physical
Hobbies

Religion
Lifestyle

When you have completed your list of life dreams, I want you to write out your retirement dreams.

My retirement dreams are:

____

____

____

____

____

Now that you have a good idea of how you want to spend your retirement years, complete the following lifeline. Draw a vertical line under "retirement age" and write the age at which you will retire.

We all know that we won't live forever. As much as we don't like to think about it, I would like you to write the age at which you think you will die on the extreme right of the line, under the word "die."

Your Lifeline

Indicate Age

Born	Present	Retirement	Die?

|____|

Age 0

You notice that the lifeline starts at age 0, when you were born, and now you have an indication of when it may end. Next, draw a vertical line through the lifeline scale at your present age and write that age below it.

Then scribble out the past, everything between age 0 and your present age. There is nothing you can do about this period. It is gone. The only thing those years represent is your experience.

How much time do you have left to accomplish what you want out of life?

____

How much time do you have prior to retirement?

____

Today is the first day of the rest of your life! I encourage you to make the best of the time remaining. Be aware of your lifeline, where you are in it, and how much time you have left to make things happen.

Now, imagine that you have just been infected with a deadly virus and you have only six months to live. Too many people wait for retirement or notice of illness to actually do the things they always wanted to do, but never did. If you only had six months left to live, how would you want to spend your remaining time?

Write out your answers here:

____

Now, go back to your list of dreams and circle or highlight the most important dreams listed that you would like to realize in your remaining time.

You have done your homework and completed all the exercises. You know who you are and what you want. Now it is time to take what you have done and put your work into a structure that will enable you to live your dreams and enjoy the future you so desire.

As mentioned earlier, when I was twenty-two and spent a "sick" day at home writing out my dreams, I started to feel great. Twenty-four hours later they were all down on paper. A couple of days later I wondered how I could possibly organize those dreams. I sat there and thought.

It then came to me. If I could position all "like" dreams together, I could identify this grouping with a name that would provide a form or organization—hence, grouping and categorizing.

Once I had all my dreams grouped and categorized by name, things were easier to see. As I looked at my accomplishments, I saw something that really woke me up. It was the realization that I really could "make it happen," as the first steps of my life plan were now staring me in the face.

Quickly, I realized that most of my category dreams were linked to each other. I realized that by numbering each dream in order of priority, the action would then lead to the accomplishment of another dream in the same or different category. As I started to number my dreams, a plan became evident (hence, prioritizing).

In the last chapter, "Know What You Want," you listed a lot of dreams, desires and expectations. Now, I would like you to go back to your dreams and group them by activity type and categorize each group by giving it a title.

For example, you might decide that your dreams cluster under headings that may include travel, family, career and finances.

In the following pages there are charts in which you can categorize your dreams. Refer back to your dream list in the last chapter and decide on your category titles. Write those titles on the charts in your workbook.

Then go back to your main list and select the dreams that fall into each category. You can do this with a different color of highlighter for each category. Then write those dreams on the category chart.

You can be brief here because you will expand on your dreams when you create a goal logbook in an upcoming chapter.

Complete your category chart now. When done, I will explain the prioritizing.

Now that you have your categories organized with your relative list of dreams, the next step is to prioritize their contents under the P next to the dream list. Which one of all the dreams takes priority? Identify it as #1 under the P column. Alternatively, which is the first if you were to follow a chronological sequence?

Go to your category chart again and do this within each category and prioritize under the P to the left of the Dream list and come back to me when you are done so that I can explain the P on the left of the category.

When I was at this stage and looking at my different categories, I noticed that some of my dreams listed under career, family, financial and travel categories were interrelated. I realized that if I secured the type of job I desired with national responsibility, I would realize other dreams, and answered my earlier question on why I go to work.

For example, securing that job would pay me $X and would satisfy a financial desire. In turn, it would allow me to get a mortgage to purchase or build a home—a family desire. It would also allow me to get the personal development training that I wanted, in my personal category, and it would allow me to travel Canada on expenses, satisfying my travel desire priority. The only category that was not satisfied was "business," and so I decided to work on that on weekends.

Now, take the time to review your categories and prioritize them. Which category is the most important to you today? Which one is your first step? Label that #1. Which ones would be nice to have, but less important? Assign those a lower priority.

Go ahead and complete prioritizing your categories and come back to me when you are done.

Now view the categories from a planning or performance point of view. Should the numbering change because of fulfillment logic? If so, change them. Which category is the most important, most logical or the one that will get the wheels rolling? In my case it was career, as noted earlier, and all the other top dreams within each category flowed from it.

Now place your dreams on a timeline. Go back and review the list you just made. To the right of each dream, based on its priority, write the date (or your age) by which you would like to have this dream realized.

Once you have done this, describe in detail your top three dreams for each time period. These will be the dreams you will work on in the next chapter, and until you make them a reality.

Group (dream list), Categorize and Prioritize (P)

P	Category	P	Dream List	Date/Age
______	____________	______	__________________	______________
		______	__________________	______________
		______	__________________	______________
		______	__________________	______________
		______	__________________	______________
		______	__________________	______________
		______	__________________	______________
		______	__________________	______________

P	Category	P	Dream List	Date/Age
______	____________	______	__________________	______________
		______	__________________	______________
		______	__________________	______________
		______	__________________	______________
		______	__________________	______________
		______	__________________	______________
		______	__________________	______________
		______	__________________	______________

P	Category	P	Dream List	Date/Age
______	____________	______	__________________	______________
		______	__________________	______________
		______	__________________	______________

P	Category	P	Dream List	Date/Age

P	Category	P	Dream List	Date/Age

P	Category	P	Dream List	Date/Age

Are You Willing to Pay the Price?

Ben Stein said, "*Nothing happens by itself... it all will come your way, once you understand that you have to make it come your way, by your own exertions.*"

You have the right to lunch when you pay for it. There is no free lunch. In other words, you can achieve all the dreams and desires that you listed in the previous chapters, but you must give something in exchange for them. They will not just happen.

What price are you willing to pay to accomplish your dreams?

Expect to make changes in your life: in the way you spend your time, effort and money, and in your relationships, habits, education and career. It is best to be aware of these costs up front. This way you can avoid surprises, and obtain support from the people who will be affected by your plan.

One year I asked each member of our family to write out five goals they wanted to accomplish that year. The one goal we all had in common was to build a dream home on the shores of a local river. As a family, we discussed the costs of realizing this dream.

The first cost would be the sale of our existing home. Would we get the price we wanted? Then, I would have to spend the time and effort to find the financing, architect and contractors for our new home. This would be at the cost of personal, family and career time.

Then, where would we live during the period of construction? Could we live in the boathouse on our building site? We would save rent money, but there would be a comfort cost to living in that small, unheated space.

We concluded that, in order to build the house of our dreams, we were prepared to take a small financial loss on the sale of our existing home, give up personal, family and business time, and live under difficult conditions that could affect our relationships.

We lived with the costs and accomplished our dream. We are thankful that we were aware of those costs before we chose to begin. Knowing the costs in advance, and being prepared to pay the price, eliminated most stress and allowed us to succeed. It is better to be prepared than surprised.

Now identify the costs associated on the form provided on the next page with each priority time-period dream from what you wrote in the last chapter. I will see you in our next chapter titled SMART goals

Are you prepared to pay the price to live your dreams? If not, consider your options. Now it is your turn to accomplish your dream. Start with the top-priority dream you chose to achieve.

Dream ____

In order to accomplish this dream I realize that there will be costs. The costs will be:

Time ____

Effort ____
____

Relationships ____
____

Habits ____
____

Career ____
____

Education____

Money ____

Other____
____

SMART Goals

How should you phrase your goals? Goals must be SMART—Specific, Measurable, Attainable, Relevant and Trackable to a Timetable. Let's look at each of these elements in detail.

S. Goals must be specific. Words like "happiness" or "success" are too vague. Ask yourself: What exactly do I want to do, be or have? For example, let's say you are getting too close to weighing 200 pounds and you want to reduce to 185 pounds within six months. You could write: In order to be healthier and more energetic, I will lose fourteen pounds within the next six months, starting today, and maintain a weight of 185 pounds from that point on.

M. Is your goal measurable? How will you know you have achieved your goal?

A Is it attainable? Give yourself a chance to succeed. Take little steps and succeed. Success breeds success.

R. Is it relevant? Would the attainment of the goal be worthwhile to you? Before you can answer this question you need to know what kind of life you want.

T. Is there a way of tracking your performance on a timetable? How do you know you are getting closer to your goal? Select dates when you will measure your progress against the milestones in your plan. You will either re-affirm that you are on track or make adjustments.

Consider the following as you set each goal:

Is this goal really mine? Am I doing this for myself or somebody else? If you are doing it for somebody else, you are not living a life of your choosing.

Is it morally right and fair?

Are my short-range goals consistent with my long-range goals? Keep in mind where you want to be ten to twenty years from now.

Can I commit myself to completing the project? If not, don't set yourself up for failure and disappointment. Save the goal for a time in your life when you can commit to making the effort.

Can I visualize myself reaching this goal? If you can't see it, it won't happen. Henry Ford said it best, "*Whether you think you can or you think you can't, you're absolutely right.*"

Creating a Goal Log

> *"When you know what your specific objectives are concerning your distant, immediate and intermediate goals, you will be more apt to recognize that which will help you achieve them."*
>
> **—W. Clement Stone**

In this chapter you are going to learn how to complete a goal log, step by step. So, find the goal log at the end of this chapter and let's get started.

First we will complete a short-range goal log together, and then on your own you can complete additional short-, medium- and long-range goal logs as per the categories you identified earlier.

Take a moment now and write out one of your goals on the sample "goal log" page at the end of this chapter. You can also complete the exercises on blank sheets of paper.

1. Setting SMART Goals

Once you have it written out, review it to see if the goal is SMART Remember, to be SMART it must be specific (well defined or described) measurable, attainable, realistic and trackable (to a specific date).

For example, I remember doing a workshop and a participant had the following goal: "to build a cottage by May." I asked if she felt it was SMART. The group started to analyze her goal. They all started to ask her questions about size, exterior and interior finish, location and more. Before long that goal was revised to: "to build and move into a 1,500-square-foot luxury post-and-beam cottage featuring hardwood floors, low maintenance and a southern exposure toward the lake at Mont Tremblant, Quebec, by May 30, 2015." It could have been even more specific, but this made the goal much clearer.

Be as descriptive as possible. Understand or define the meaning of each word used. You want to create as clear a picture as you possibly can in as few words as possible.

Take your time to write out your goal, as SMART as possible, in your goal logbook now and when you are completed, come back and join me here for the next step.

2. Date for Completion

From the first day in hospital I had set myself goals. I had promised myself I would be out of that Stryker bed for my birthday, August 26, and I was.

—Rick Hansen

The next step is to add a completion date for each of your goals. Be the master of those dates, not the slave. Don't abandon your goals; just change the deadlines if you have to. Self-motivation and personal leadership include the ability to distinguish between defeat and setback.

Turn to your goal logbook now and write in a realistic deadline for your goal. You will lay out the milestones toward these dates later in your action plan. Come back and join me when you are done

3. Outcomes

Chance favors the prepared mind.

—Louis Pasteur

Next is the outcome—the result you want, expressed in detail. State your outcomes in positive, sensory-based terms: the sights, sounds and feelings you want to experience. For example, look at the weight-reduction goal: "Within six months, I will weigh 185 pounds." I see myself slimmer, my clothes fit better and I am more attractive. I hear the opening of the storage box of clothes that had gotten too tight, people giving me compliments on my weight, saying how good I look and asking me how I did it. I feel energized, healthy and active."

Take a few moments now and imagine four things you will see, hear and feel when you have completed your goal. See, feel and hear yourself as being at the completion stage of that goal. Write them in the goal log now and when completed, come back and join me.

4. Possible Obstacles

Obstacles are those frightful things you see when you take your eyes off your goal.

—Henry Ford

The next task is to identify the obstacles that could stand in your way. What events or circumstances might make it difficult to reach your goal? How will you handle those roadblocks? It is better to identify them now and have alternate plans ready than to be caught by surprise.

Take the time now to list all the obstacles that you might encounter. Once you have done this for each of your goals, go back and prepare your contingency plans. "If this happened, I would…" Be ready.

Allow me to share an incident that occurred in my life that led me to identifying obstacles and contingency plans in advance on all of my goals.

Just before turning thirty, I was employed with Canada's second largest land developer and experiencing a high level of success. I was responsible for over 10,000 acres of commercial, industrial and residential land in the National Capital Region. I also sold a lot of their land in Aylmer and Gatineau, Quebec. I was the only one selling at the time. It got to the point where licensed real estate agents reported me to the Quebec Real Estate Board. I was investigated and learned a lot about what is allowed and what is not. The conclusion was that as long as I was selling land for a developer, I didn't need a real estate license.

Within weeks Canada's largest land developer approached me to ask if I would consider selling for them too. They suggested I leave and take on a contract with my existing employer and with them. I always wanted to be in business for myself and

I figured that this would be the time, as we only had one young child. I approached my employer and obtained their support.

So I left the security of the corporate world to go into business for myself, selling residential lots in West Quebec. Both of Canada's largest land developers and builders were getting out of the new-house construction market in the early 1980s. Real estate just wasn't selling. Interest rates were at an all-time high and a separatist government was in power in Quebec.

Immediately after going into business for myself, I started on a plan. The plan was to prepare the lots for a mass sale six weeks before an upcoming provincial election. During the period preceding the sale, I had the lots bulldozed, picketed and signed with lot numbers, dimensions and phone numbers.

Finally, the time arrived. I expected big results, and being the proactive guy that I am, I started to investigate commercial land development opportunities. The marketing kicked in, as did the support from the local media. Within five days, I had sold over 100 individual lots and earned just over $80,000 in commissions. Not a bad week after being in business for only six months.

Having expected this to happen, I had exercised an option to purchase some commercial land and went to work on it immediately. I was creating a major tourist attraction, and spent $100,000 within the next twenty days preparing the site.

By the time thirty days rolled around, suppliers were looking for money. I was wondering what happened to mine. I called the office of Canada's largest land developer. There was no answer. I drove into town and visited their office, only to learn that it was closed down and everyone I knew had been let go. I would have to direct my inquiries to a vice-president located in head office in Toronto.

Before long, I met with that VP. After hearing me out, he said he liked me and would give me $5,000. Otherwise, go play in the traffic. He felt he wasn't obliged to pay me because I was not a licensed real estate agent. I could not believe what he was saying. I decided to refuse his offer and seek legal advice based on the experience I gained from being previously investigated.

Because of a very simple obstacle that could have been identified in advance (with a contingency plan put in place), my "success" became a nightmare.

All five goals that were well in line for accomplishment experienced a major setback. First, I was obliged to pay my suppliers. I went to the local bank and borrowed $10,000 at a 22 percent interest rate. In the end, I had borrowed twenty $10,000 loans at 22 percent interest. My mortgage came up for renewal at 19 percent and my lawyer advised me to give him $25,000 up front for court costs or move out of our dream home and into an apartment in Ottawa to avoid Ontario Supreme Court costs. That hurt the most. My wife, Joan, was pregnant with our second child, David, and was looking forward to raising our children at home. We moved out, rented out our home and found an apartment in town.

Not long after that, I had no choice but to close down the business I had started. I was now in significant debt. Fortunately I landed a job and slowly began to rebuild. Within three years, Canada's largest land developer settled out of court and I secured all monies due to me. I got myself back on my feet again, and ended up in a better position because of the experience.

However, there is no need to go through what I went through. If I had only addressed one possible obstacle: what if they decide not to pay me?

Had I even thought of it, I would have waited for the money to be in my hands before proceeding into further investment. That would have been my contingency plan.

Mind you, I do have a "do-it-now" attitude and don't usually take the time to think about everything that can go wrong. I learn by doing and adjusting as need be. You don't want to think about obstacles for too long, because it will delay you in your actions. Identify the most obvious and potentially most serious ones that come to mind and move on.

5. Contingency Plans

> *Success comes to those who set goals and pursue them regardless of obstacles and disappointments.*
>
> **—Napoleon Hill**

Based on the possible obstacles you have identified, what can you do in advance to prepare? If that obstacle caught you by surprise, it could knock you down. If you have a contingency plan, you will stand tall and recognize it as just a bump along the road to success. You put into action your contingency plan and move on. You just saved yourself two steps in the process—one being knocked down and the other getting back up. Don't let it take three years out of your life as it did to me.

Take the time now to identify some possible contingency plans to obstacles you identified earlier. "If this happened, I would..."

When done, come back and join me.

6. Skills and Behaviors Required

> *Almost every goal you set for yourself involves learning. The ability to learn what you need to know, in a hurry, is the basic tool for getting what you want.*
>
> **—Joyce Brothers**

What skills will you require for you to achieve your goal? How, where and when will you learn those skills?

Behavior can be defined as the way you conduct yourself. Will you need to change your behavior in order to put your skills into action?

For example, when we laid out our goal to build our dream home, I needed to acquire some design and construction skills. Not so much the "to do" skills but rather an understanding of them in order to negotiate and inspect the hired skills. So I made it a goal to take a course on building your own home, which turned out to be invaluable.

I developed my behaviors, too. I researched designs and materials. I read up on things, spoke to many contractors, and made sure I was on top of everything. I learned how to accept criticism and provide constructive feedback to the tradesmen, maintain a positive attitude and to persist until the job got done.

Take the time now to identify some of the skills and behaviors you will require, and come back and join me when you are done.

7. People, Groups or Resources Required

> *In order to reach your ultimate goal, you must form a group of people with ambitions like your own, but differing in specialized knowledge. Together, the group can solve problems that no one person alone could solve.*
>
> **—Napoleon Hill**

You can accomplish only so much on your own. You can achieve much more by calling on the help of different people, groups or resources. Regardless of your goal, you will attain it with much less difficulty if you ally yourself with others. Some people create mastermind groups; others create an advisory board; others consult with their friends and families while others benefit from membership in an association. It is through others that we sometimes get our best ideas. The best results come from an organized effort of two or more people working toward a definite outcome.

What individuals or groups of people could help you? What resources can you call on? List them now.

For example, while completing the log for my goal to become a speaker, I wanted to become part of a professional speaking association, so I joined the Canadian Association of Professional Speakers. I felt I needed an individual to help fast-track me into the business, internationally. The timing was right and I found Denis Cauvier, right in my own town. When I looked for a speech coach to provide me with constructive feedback, I found Velma Latmore, a person who has dedicated her life to effective communications through Toastmasters. I also needed resource material, so I reorganized my office and got out all the books that had inspired me over the years. I began researching using the Internet and visiting bookstores regularly.

8. Action Plan

> *Say three times 'This one thing I do,' emphasizing the word one. One step at a time will get you there much more surely than haphazardly leaping and jumping. It is the steady pace, the consistent speed that leads to the most efficient start to your destination.*
>
> **—Dr. Norman Vincent Peale**

An action plan is a step-by-step outline of the tasks that lead to the achievement of a goal. Treat each action step as a sub-goal.

What do you need to do to turn your goals into reality? Establish a logical sequence of steps. Prioritize them and place a target date for accomplishment beside each activity. By dating each step along the way you can monitor and measure your progress and reward yourself accordingly.

Acknowledge the events beyond your control upon which goal results depend. Identify the areas where you will co-ordinate your actions with other people, in order to get the support you need, when you need it.

Identifying the actions you need to take, and the schedule for those actions, makes all the difference between a wish and a realistic, achievable goal. The main objective is to set up your action plan in a way that guarantees you success. By this I mean create an action plan that is full of little steps taken one at a time so that you can experience success along the way. Too many people just identify gigantic steps, steps that turn out to be unrealistic or unachievable in the time frames allocated. They soon sense that they can't do it and then give up. Don't do that to yourself.

Create an action plan that is set up for success, little steps at a time. Experience your success daily. You can't realize your tomorrow's dream without first taking a small step forward today toward its realization.

For example, twenty years ago I laid out a three-phase action plan to build a waterfront home for my family. The first phase was to learn about the local real estate. Over the first ten to fifteen years I acquired a good understanding of land, and when riverfront properties finally became available I found the perfect lot.

The next phase was to pay off and prepare the land. Over a period of five years I cleared the trees, put in the driveway, fixed the shoreline, built a boathouse, and put in a septic bed, a flower garden and grass. The property was ready. The only thing missing was the house.

The third and concluding phase (the last two years) was to design the house, to sell our old home, acquire the financing and build. One step at a time, we accomplished a dream that went back twenty years.

Take the time now to list all the necessary steps to accomplish each of your goals. Use extra paper if you need it. This is the most important stage in creating your goal log. Take the time to list everything that comes to mind. When you are done, review your list and identify the steps in order of priority. Spend a lot of time in this area before moving on. Identify everything right down to the little steps and set yourself up for success.

When you are done, come back here.

9. Methods of Monitoring and Measuring Progress

> *Goals are not only absolutely necessary to motivate us. They are essential to really keep us alive.*
>
> **—Robert H. Schuller**

Knowing how you are doing will motivate you to keep going. How will you monitor your behavior and measure your progress? Think of some ways in which you can do this on an ongoing basis. Monitoring will allow you to recognize your progress and reward yourself accordingly. It will also warn you to take corrective action should you find you are not following your plan.

How can you make sure you are on track? What sort of measurements can you take regularly? Fill in that part of your log now and come back here when you are done.

At the end of chapter 9, "Monitoring and Measure Your Progress," I will provide you with a Monthly Monitor Chart that you can use to monitor your daily progress.

10. The Reward (What's in it for me?)

I feel the greatest reward for doing is the opportunity to do more.

—Jonas Salk

How are you going to reward yourself when you accomplish your goal? You deserve something besides the achievement of that goal. Visualize the rewards you'll give yourself. Also, decide how you can pay yourself along the way. It will be easier to keep up the good work when you periodically reward yourself.

What are the things you really enjoy? Plan to treat yourself to some of these things after you complete each action step. This way you will practice discipline—doing what you have to do even when you don't want to—and accomplish your goals at the same time. Remember that action that gets rewarded gets repeated.

For example, I like to play golf with clients on Friday afternoons. I usually take some time on Sunday evenings to plan out my week in relation to my monthly goals. I identify the times during the week where I have family and business commitments, and then I fill in my schedule with activities that will help me reach my goals for that month. Before long my schedule is full. By the time Friday rolls around, I either reward myself by playing golf, because I did everything I indicated that I would, or I punish myself and stay in the office and do everything that I didn't do.

Imagine if I rewarded myself for something I indicated that I would do, but then didn't do. Do you think I would have a good game of golf? I don't think so. I would be feeling kind of guilty. However, imagine how well I would play golf, and how much more I would enjoy the game, if it were a reward for doing what I indicated to myself that I would do.

You can use dinners, movies, vacations, clothes, events or whatever you enjoy as a reward. Tie the required disciplines to something you really enjoy and treat these enjoyments as a reward for doing what you indicated you would do. Stop treating yourself to these enjoyments for absolutely no reason, and you will soon be a master of discipline.

Discipline is the key. Discipline is a commitment to yourself to do what you have to do, even when you don't want to do it. As discipline gets recognized and rewarded it gets repeated and becomes a matter of habit.

Take the time now to list your rewards and come back here when you are done.

Before I go on to the final step of the goal log, you should now take the time to complete goal logs for your additional short-, medium- and long-range goals identified in the earlier chapter, "Group, Categorize and Prioritize." Take your time, as it is well worth the effort to do it now, while it is fresh in your head. When they are complete, come back here.

11. Commitment

> *There is not much use climbing the ladder part way. People who succeed have the single-minded devotion to their goal that is best described as total commitment. They have the ability and desire to work to top capacity.*
>
> **—Joyce Brothers**

This is where you make a commitment to yourself. Commitment is defined as an agreement or pledge to do something in the future.

You have identified everything relating to the accomplishment of a goal. You've identified possible obstacles and are prepared for the worst-case scenario. "If only" doesn't exist. Blaming others is a thing of the past. You have taken control of your life and your attitude. You are disciplined. Only you are responsible for your future.

Are you serious about accomplishing the goals you just outlined?

Are you committed to following through?

If you are, sign the pledge at the bottom of your goal logbook now.

You are now making the biggest commitment you will ever make—a commitment to yourself, the most important person in the world.

Of all commitments, the ones you make to yourself are the most important to respect. If you can't keep a commitment to yourself, you can't succeed.

Sign the pledge at the bottom of your goal logbook now and I will see you in the next chapter.

Goal Log

Creation Date: ____________________ Last Updated Date: ________________

Identify Goal: ____

____

____

Deadline / Date:____

Outcome: ____

A. What will I see when I get there?

1. ____
2. ____
3. ____

B. What sounds will I hear?

1. ____
2. ____
3. ____

C. What will I feel?

1. ____
2. ____
3. ____

D. Possible Obstacles / Contingency Plan

1. ____
2. ____
3. ____

E. Skills and behaviors required

1. ____
2. ____
3. ____

F. Identify people, groups or resources required

1. ____
2. ____
3. ____

G. Action Plan with Dates:

Action #1: ____

Start: ________________________Finish: ________________________

Action #2: ____

Start: ______________________ Finish: ______________________

Action #3: ____

Start: ______________________ Finish: ______________________

Action #4: ____

Start: ______________________ Finish: ______________________

Action #5: ____

Start: ______________________ Finish: ______________________

H. Methods of monitoring and measuring progress

____

____

____

I. Reward, what's in it for me?

____

____

____

J. I have committed myself to the accomplishment of this goal by:

____

Signature: ______________________________ Date: ______________

Taking Action

This is where the magic begins. By having a focus, and taking steps to success daily, you start to feel good about yourself and your accomplishments. You wake up each morning thankful for another day, because you are going to do something today to bring your dream a little step closer to reality, and you are going to congratulate yourself for having done it.

It all begins with you becoming action oriented. You need a do-it-now attitude. The first two letters of goal are "go." Now is the time to get going. Don't tell the world what you can do—show it! It is in the doing that things get done.

Avoid procrastination. Procrastination is the process of habitually putting things off. It is tempting to make excuses… "I don't have the time," "I think they said they were going to be in meetings all day, so I didn't call," or "This could take forever; I'll do it when I have a spare day."

Procrastination will cause you to miss deadlines, leading to lost opportunities and income, lower productivity and wasted time. It will lower your motivation, heighten your stress and generate frustration and anger. Is this the way you want to live?

Take control of your life now! Reverse the procrastination habit by being as clever about completing things as you have been about putting them off.

Don't expect to find time to achieve your goals. The only way to get time is to make time. Start by committing to a do-it-now mentality. A do-it-now mentality makes you a self-starter—a person who can recognize a need and take appropriate action without waiting to be told to. As a self-starter, you will avoid the pressure, frustration and anxiety that come from having others tell you what and how to do things. You exercise your creativity in solving problems and doing work. As a result, you are more productive.

As you take maximum advantage of every opportunity, your sense of timing sharpens. You seldom miss something you want because of being late. Your services become more eagerly sought after.

This type of do-it-now attitude will also help you overcome your resistance to dealing with unpleasant tasks. Don't delay your gratification by delaying the unpleasant tasks. By tackling them first, you get them over with and can get on with the more pleasant things in life.

With an action-oriented, do-it-now attitude you get more out of your day. When you complete the unpleasant or hard jobs first and you act on the big tasks, little bites at a time, you'll trim your anxiety and stress load while gaining self-respect and self-confidence. After you apply this type of discipline long enough, you will establish a routine and make a new habit. Human behavior studies suggest that if you do something every day for twenty-one days, it will become a habit. Be consciously action oriented for the next twenty-one days and you will master procrastination.

Here are some action-oriented techniques to apply each day:

Determine your most productive time of the day and dedicate it to "Me" time. "Me" time is for you to do whatever you have to do that will bring you closer to achieving your goals. It may be as simple as visualizing the accomplishment of your goals or doing what you have to do, for you.

The point here is to dedicate at least one hour of the most productive time to the most important person in the world, and after completing that hour, reward yourself. Remember, any behavior that gets recognized and/or rewarded gets repeated.

Manage your goals. You have already set your goals and action plans and have prioritized the actions. Take your annual goals and break them down into quarters;

break quarters into months, months into weeks and, finally, weeks into days, and define your daily disciplines.

Do the same with each day's activities. Break the large tasks down into small, manageable pieces. Try to accomplish some of these pieces each day. Before long, you will have accomplished a large task.

End each day by writing a prioritized to-do list for the next day. At the end of each week and month do the same for the next week and month. Get organized. Use a daily planner. You will be better organized if you write down everything.

Clear your mind of clutter. Solve problems while they are small. Whatever you do, do it once, to the best of your ability, and move on.

Question all tasks to make sure they are worthwhile. Do the worst or hardest jobs first.

Be decisive and remove time wasters, including interruptions, from all of your activities.

Remember to take care of yourself by exercising, watching your diet, and maintaining a balance in your life.

And when evening comes and your next day's to-do list is written, celebrate. Action that gets rewarded gets repeated. Do this for the next 30 days and you will be transformed into an action-oriented, do-it-now person.

Be proactive. An action-oriented person is proactive. When you are proactive, you have initiative—you can see a need, figure out how to best satisfy it, determine the appropriate time to take the right action, and proceed. When you are proactive, you lead. When you lead, you take control of yourself and get the things you want out of life.

Use visualization techniques. Make visualization a daily discipline. Visualize in order to actualize your goals.

As you see the picture in your mind and feel it, you are bringing yourself to a place of believing you now have it. You are also invoking trust and faith in the Universe, because you are focusing on the end result and experiencing the feeling of that, without giving any attention whatsoever to "how" it will come about. Your mind is seeing the picture as done. Your mind and your entire state of being are seeing it as already done. That is the art of visualization.

When you visualize, you generate powerful thoughts and feelings of having it now. The law of attraction then returns that reality to you, just as you saw it in your mind. The mind itself cannot tell the difference. Imagination is everything. It is the preview of life's coming attractions.

Try using visualization to help yourself become action oriented. When you set your goals, you pictured something that you wanted to have, be or do. Everything we have or do is preceded by an image in our mind. Visualization is seeing the end result. It is a form of mental rehearsal. Through the use of imagination, what you see is what you will get.

Your vision of your goals must be clear. There is a difference between "dreaming" about having something in the future and "visualizing" having it in the future. The power to believe makes the difference. Visualizing implies a structured and disciplined view of what you are trying to accomplish. Through visualization you picture yourself already in possession of your goal. By visualizing you look at your goal from many different viewpoints. By examining your goal from all of the viewpoints, you see the situation clearly and can act on the aspects that will result in the greatest payback.

Go put your creed into your deed.

—Ralph Waldo Emerson

Forget all your inhibitions. See things as you want them to be, not as they are. Take time to sit back, close your eyes, and see yourself accomplishing your goal. You are watching a movie based on the success that you have become. Focus your attention on the results. See yourself there. Feel the emotions. See the colors, the details; hear the sounds.

If you form a clear and detailed picture of your future, ways and means of getting it will be revealed to you. Keep focusing on what you want, not on how you will do it. The laws of nature will take over. The more you visualize, the more resources you will attract. Your vision will act as a magnet. It will attract people, events and circumstances to it. It is a self-fulfilling prophecy.

And when you're having a difficult moment during the day, take the time to visualize the accomplishment of your goal. It will refocus and relax you, and the issue of the moment will matter less. The major incident of today will probably be insignificant in the future. Don't trip over molehills.

Try visualizing right now. Project yourself six months into the future. Select one of your short-range goals. Now get comfortable and close your eyes. See yourself accomplishing your goal. You are now successfully there. You made it; you're living and breathing it. Use your imagination. See all the details, hear the sounds, feel the emotions, and celebrate. Visualize this for the next five minutes. Focus on the success.

I recommend that you get into the habit of doing this daily. Your enthusiastic attitude about your vision will not only keep you motivated, but it will also get others excited about your dream.

Control Yourself. Just as thoughts can control feelings and feelings control behavior, the reverse is also true.

If you change your behavior you can change your feelings and ultimately your thoughts. *It is not how you feel that determines how you act; it is how you act that determines how you feel.* For example, if you pull your shoulders back, lift your head high, force yourself to smile and cheerfully greet others, you will find your mood changing.

The same process applies to self-talk. Feed your mind negative thoughts and it will produce negative actions. Feed your mind positive, confident information and your mind will react in kind. You cannot completely control the circumstances around you, but you can control what you say to yourself and how you think.

These easy-to-do techniques are the daily steps that will lead you to success. Each success breeds success. There will be obstacles along the way, and when they get in your way, be ready for them. You must persist. Stick to it. You will get things done, and meet your objectives and goals. Keep in mind that often when we are ready to quit, success lies just around the corner. Don't ever give up on taking action. Make your dreams happen!

Monitoring and Measuring Your Progress

Are you doing what you set out to do?

If so, are you rewarding yourself for your accomplishments?

If not, are you revising your plan?

Knowing how you're doing will motivate you to keep going and to make the necessary adjustments along the way. At the end of this chapter, you will find two charts that will be helpful to you in monitoring your actions and behaviors.

The first one is a **Soar Chart.**

Here's the way the Soar Chart works. You take the goal categories that you identified in the chapter on grouping, categorizing and prioritizing, and on the Soar Chart write each category name in the column under the title "Goals."

Then, on the line beside each category, briefly write out the goals for each time period. Although the chart shows time periods of Years 1, 3, 5 and long-term, you may use whatever time periods you prefer, as long as you are specific with your dates. I use a six-month period for my short-range goals. I use January 1 as a beginning of a new year and my birthday in March as the beginning of a new age, so some of my goals are related to calendar periods and others are related to age.

I use the three- and five-year columns for my medium-range goals and the "long-term column" for my retirement and whole-life goals.

The beauty of the Soar Chart is that it summarizes all the expectations and dreams that you intend to turn into reality. Your completed Soar Chart reminds you of what is truly important in your life. It reinforces your expectations and gives you a boost in down times. It helps you in your visualization process. It is your roadmap to your future, but with specific dates or ages.

Use this chart daily, when you wake up, sit in traffic or wait on someone. When you are reading your Soar Chart, reviewing your goals and visualizing their accomplishment, you are projecting your mind into a time of happiness and success by visualizing goal accomplishment. It's easy, fun and rewarding. Remember, your thoughts of today are your tomorrow.

My Soar Chart is with me at all times. I review it regularly, add to it as I go, and update it every six months, or as need be. My Soar Chart has kept me focused on what is important to me.

Take the time now and fill in your Soar Chart, but be brief, as space is limited. Write down your categories and goals under the appropriate time periods. Fill in what you can now, and come back to me when you are done.

The **Monthly Monitor Chart** provides you with a method to monitor your behaviors and activities.

Across the top of the chart are the numbers 1 to 31. These are for each day of the month. You can see today's date, so you can start today; you do not have to wait until the first of the month. There is no use procrastinating, do it now!

Down the side of the chart is a list of daily activities. First is the Goal Review with a line for morning, noon and night. The idea is to review your goals from your goal chart in the morning when you wake up, at midday and before going to bed at night. If you reviewed your goals in the morning, give yourself a check mark in the column under that day's date. If not, leave it blank. As you know, it takes twenty-one consecutive days to make something a habit.

This method also works for the accomplishments of goals. However, we are human and we have a tough time doing things for twenty-one consecutive days, so the trick here is to get at least twenty-five check marks over a thirty-one-day period to make it a habit, a discipline, a reality.

Now let me ask you some questions. If you were to review your goals three times a day for the next thirty-one days, what do you think would happen to your life? Do you think you may become more focused? Would you manage your time better and get more out of each day? Would you be more action oriented? Would you eventually realize your dreams and live the life you so desire?

I don't think so; I know so. The Monthly Monitor Chart has proven itself worldwide time and time again.

In the next section of the Monthly Monitor Chart, under activities, are daily affirmations that should also be reviewed and put into action each day.

First is "I recognize and praise." Did you take the time today to look at the good you do? Did you build yourself up or did you beat yourself up?

What you do, or give, to yourself is what you do, or give, to others. You can only give away what you have inside to give.

So, first give yourself a check mark if you recognized and praised yourself today. Did you also recognize and praise others? If so, give yourself a double check mark. If not, leave it blank. Do the same for each of the other affirmations listed. Mind you, you can change these affirmations to whatever you want to affirm each day.

Now look at "Goals" on the Monthly Monitor Chart. Here you will list your top three goals for that month. Under each goal, identify three daily actions toward the accomplishment of that goal. These actions could be something you'll repeat daily or weekly, or do only once. Write down what you think you can accomplish. Take time now to complete your Monthly Monitor Chart now and come back here when you are done.

Let's summarize. The Soar Chart summarizes your short- and long-range goals, and the Monthly Monitor Chart details what you plan to do each day and month. Combined back-to-back on one piece of paper that can be folded and placed in your pocket, wallet or purse, they will serve as a great tool to your success.

The charts will remind, discipline, guide, monitor and reward you. They will make you more aware of your behaviors, pointing out when you should make adjustments. Now that the charts are completed, carry them with you at all times. Refer to them at least three times a day. Fill in the Monthly Monitor daily and revise it monthly. The effort you make using these charts will help you make your goals your reality.

The Soar Chart

Goals	Year 1	Year 3	Year 5	Long Term

Overall Purpose / Mission:

____

____

____

MONTHLY MONITOR CHART ™

ACTIVITIES	1	2	3	4	5	6	7	8	9	10	11	12	13	14	15	16	17	18	19	20	21	22	23	24	25	26	27	28	29	30	31
Goal Review																															
A.M.																															
Noon																															
P.M.																															
I recognize and praise																															
I visualize and use imagery																															
I talk positively to myself																															
I am an empathetic listener																															
I am patient and I probe																															
Goal #1 ______																															
Actions 1. ______																															
2. ______																															
3. ______																															
Goal #2 ______																															
Actions 1. ______																															
2. ______																															
3. ______																															
Goal #3 ______																															
Actions 1. ______																															
2. ______																															
3. ______																															

Summary

- Why do you go to work? Question the answer and find the truth.
- Why set goals? What is in it for you?
- Group, categorize and prioritize your dreams.
- Be prepared to pay a price to make your dreams a reality, but are you willing to pay the price?
- A goal is an end, a result, not just a task to be performed.
- Goals are an extension of your values.
- Goals must be SMART—Specific, Measurable, Attainable, Relevant and Trackable to a Timetable.
- Ask yourself: Is this goal really mine? Is it morally right and fair? Are my short-range goals consistent with my long-range goals? Can I commit myself to complete the project? Can I visualize myself reaching this goal?
- Create a goal logbook and address each of the following areas:
    - ◊ State the goal, date for completion and outcomes expressed in sensory-based terms—the sights, sounds and feelings you want to experience.
    - ◊ Identify obstacles you might meet, develop the contingency plans to overcome those possible obstacles, identify the skills and behaviors you'll need, and the people, groups or resources you can call on for help.
    - ◊ Develop a detailed step-by-step success-oriented action plan with start and finish dates, and with a method of monitoring and measuring your progress.
    - ◊ Create a system to recognize and reward yourself for doing what you indicated you would do along the way.
    - ◊ Finally, make a commitment to yourself to follow through and do what you have to do.

Take action, take control and avoid procrastination. Visualize in order to actualize your dreams. Determine your most productive time of the day and discipline yourself to make it your time.

Manage your goals, be decisive, proactive and clear your mind of clutter.

Use the Soar Chart and the Monthly Monitor Chart to stay focused and to monitor your daily disciplines.

BEHAVIOR TOWARD YOUR ORGANIZATION

Organizational Goals

Now that you know how to set goals and create a goal log for yourself, it should be a lot easier for you to go through the same process with your objectives at work. As I mentioned earlier, in most organizations, management devotes enormous energy to setting work objectives and conducting performance reviews for individual employees. Corporations go through this time-consuming and costly exercise to ensure the most favorable results for their firm. They follow this process because they know it works. Now you too can benefit from this same process.

You know your personal goals and you have taken the time to create a goal log. In your action plan, you have identified the steps you have to take and you are taking action toward them. You probably also came to the realization that you need a job or a business to help you accomplish some of your dreams and desires. If not, you already have that job or business and are going to work for a reason, *your* reason.

So when you go to work, know what you expect from your job. What are the three most important things that you want from your job? If you don't know or if you can't answer this question, you are not taking control of your life or your future and you are leaving life to chance and circumstance.

I am sure your organization has three important goals that they want you to accomplish while in their employ. Should you not also make *them* aware of *your* top three goals? This is part of a win-win strategy.

Your job or business has expectations of you. You too should have expectations of your job or business in return. Make sure you know what these expectations are, and make sure the people you report to know them as well, and are in agreement. Then, together, everyone can win.

In most organizations the expectations of management for salespeople is revenue- or volume-based, while salespeople's expectations are to have the freedom and support to do their job, and to be well rewarded or recognized for doing it. You have already reviewed and determined your personal goals; now let's take a look at the organizational goals that you are expected to meet or surpass.

Do you know your revenue or volume targets? If you don't, you better find out what they are because without them you have nothing to work toward.

So the first thing we do is to set that SMART goal, as discussed earlier. Let's pretend your goal or target is to sell and deliver $1 million of new revenue within the fiscal year for your organization. How do you intend to meet it? Do you have a plan? That is what the goal log is all about. The goal log works for you at work as it does in your personal life. You go through each of the same steps as you did earlier. However, when it comes to the Action Plan portion, you have a few more steps to consider.

In detailing your action plan, you have to take history into consideration. What can the past tell you about seasonality trends, favorable market conditions, competitive activities, your call-to-close ratios, etc.? Knowing these and other sorts of information can benefit you considerably.

You should first review the past, as it is likely to repeat itself. Then map out your target as finely as you can by periods—quarters, months, weeks, days. You will find at the end of this section a chart titled the Sales Results Worksheet, broken down by month, which may be of assistance to you. Each of these periods becomes a sub-target or sub-goal and should be monitored and measured accordingly. But in order for you to meet these sub-goals, you have to do something. That something is your behavior.

As a salesperson you have to demonstrate appropriate behavior. You have to be constantly filling the funnel with suspects (potential buyers), qualifying them to become prospects, making presentations, acquiring new business to become buyers, and following up. You also have to maintain and develop more business from existing buyers, handle requests, go to meetings, complete all kinds of reports and maintain a positive and enthusiastic attitude, no matter what. You have a lot of behavior that you have to demonstrate.

However, before you do any of that, you need to clearly define your organizational goals. Take the time now to complete a goal log, as you did for personal goals, for each of your organizational goals for the fiscal year, using the sales results worksheet at the end of this chapter as a support tool to your goal log.

Then include those goals on your Soar Chart and Monthly Monitor Chart.

Goal Log

Creation Date: ____________________ Last Updated Date: ________________

Identify Goal: ____

____

____

Deadline / Date: ____

Outcome: ____

A. What will I see when I get there?

1. ____
2. ____
3. ____

B. What sounds will I hear?

1. ____
2. ____
3. ____

C. What will I feel?

1. ____
2. ____
3. ____

D. Possible Obstacles / Contingency Plan

1. ____
2. ____
3. ____

E. Skills and behaviors required

1. ______________________________
2. ______________________________
3. ______________________________

F. Identify people, groups or resources required

1. ______________________________
2. ______________________________
3. ______________________________

G. Action Plan with Dates:

Action #1: ______________________________
Start: ______________Finish: ______________
Action #2: ______________________________
Start: ______________Finish: ______________
Action #3: ______________________________
Start: ______________Finish: ______________
Action #4: ______________________________
Start: ______________Finish: ______________
Action #5: ______________________________
Start: ______________Finish: ______________

H. Methods of monitoring and measuring progress

____
____
____

I. Reward, what's in it for me?

____
____
____

J. I have committed myself to the accomplishment of this goal by:

____

Signature: ______________________Date: ____________

SALES RESULTS WORKSHEET

Sales I will obtain in the next 12 months:

Sales I will obtain broken down by month

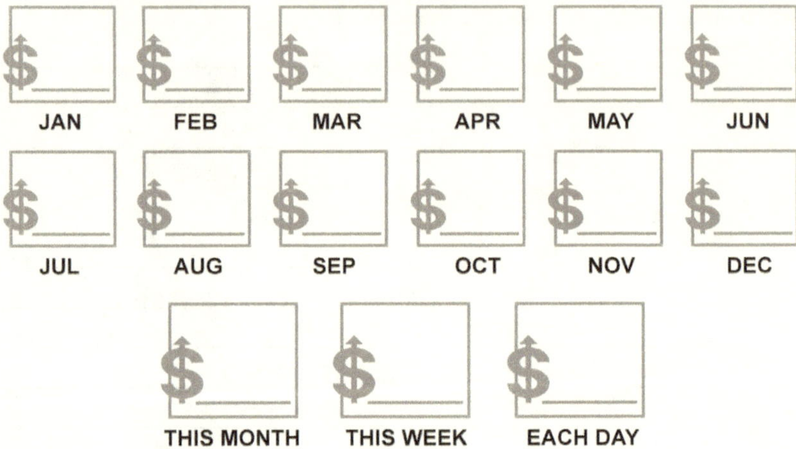

The Soar Chart

Goals	Year 1	Year 3	Year 5	Long Term

Overall Purpose / Mission:

____

____

____

MONTHLY MONITOR CHART ™

ACTIVITIES	1	2	3	4	5	6	7	8	9	10	11	12	13	14	15	16	17	18	19	20	21	22	23	24	25	26	27	28	29	30	31
Goal Review																															
A.M.																															
Noon																															
P.M.																															
I recognize and praise																															
I visualize and use imagery																															
I talk positively to myself																															
I am an empathetic listener																															
I am patient and I probe																															
Goal #1 ____________																															
Actions 1. ____________																															
2. ____________																															
3. ____________																															
Goal #2 ____________																															
Actions 1. ____________																															
2. ____________																															
3. ____________																															
Goal #3 ____________																															
Actions 1. ____________																															
2. ____________																															
3. ____________																															

Call-to-Close Ratios and Tracking Behaviors

Call-to-close ratios are used to measure performance and identify areas of improvement. When you know your call-to-close ratios, you can determine which behaviors will give you a better ROTI—return on time invested.

Call-to-close ratios basically determine the behavior in each step of the sales process from how many telephone calls you have to make to get a face-to-face appointment, how many appointments turn into a qualified presentation, how many presentations result in a sale, to the value of the sale.

To understand this better, allow me to share this Behavior Worksheet with you.

Behavior Worksheet

1. In order to generate $_____,
   I need to get in front of ____ prospects.
2. In order to get in front of ____ prospects,
   I need to book ____ appointments.
3. In order to book ____ appointments,
   I need to speak to ____ prospects.
4. In order to speak to ____ prospects,
   I need to initiate ____ points of contact.
5. To initiate ____ points of contact,

I need to: ____

____

____

____

However, if you don't know your ratios, you will first need to track your daily behaviors, which is not all that difficult and worth the effort in the long run.

Below is a Monthly Tracking Worksheet. You can modify this worksheet to fit your own particular needs.

Behavior – Monthly Tracking Worksheet

Date: ____________ Name: ______________________________________

Attempts to Contact:

Leads Provided: _______

Cold Calls: _______

Fax: _______

E-mail: _______

Dials: _______
Referrals: _______
Networking: _______
Other: ____
____
____
____

Total attempts to contact: _______

Buyers contacted (#): _______
Appointments booked (#): ____________________ Ratio: ____________________
Face to face (#): ____________________ Ratio: ____________________
Sales generated (#): ____________________ Ratio: ____________________
Sales value ($): ____________________ Ratio: ____________________

Create your own daily behavior tracking worksheet. Simply list the working days of the month down the left side of the page, 1-31. Then identify all the behaviors you engage in on a daily basis. Each day track those behaviors by occasion or time. The objective is to keep track of your daily behaviors, which are then summarized monthly to determine the time spent, and your averages, or ratios. This will in turn help you in adjusting your behaviors to achieve greater results.

Let me share an experience I once had in sales and how tracking my behaviors helped me better organize my behaviors and timing, which in turn led to more sales.

At one stage in my life I wanted to learn everything I could about franchising, so I decided to sell franchises. The franchising company would provide me with leads from advertising and inquiries received through a toll-free 1-800 number. Each day they would send me a batch of leads for follow up. From the very beginning, I decided to track my behaviors and results so that I could measure the feasibility of doing what I was doing, as I was on a full-commission structure, paid only on results.

The first thing I did was create a simple form with each day of the month down the left-hand side. Across the top I had headings that related to what I wanted to track. Because the franchises were promoted nationally and my work was related more to telephone work than face to face, I had headings such as dials, connected, left message, call # 2, fax, mailing, follow up, trip, presentation and close.

Each day as I sat down at my desk to follow up on leads, I would have my form in front of me and I would make a mark under each heading that applied to the behavior I was conducting. At the end of the week and the end of the month I would total up my behaviors and identify the ratios. After three months, I had determined my ratios. Here is what I learned:

It took 500 dials to get 300 contacts;

Out of the 300 contacts, 285 said no, leaving me with fifteen potential qualified prospects;

Out of the fifteen qualified prospects, three would take a trip to head office at their expense;

Out of three, two would buy the franchise;

My commission was $1,250 each or a total of $2,500.

What I learned from tracking my behaviors was that I would have to make 500 dials to get two sales generating a total commission of $2,500. As I dug deeper, I realized I was getting five dollars per dial. Not a bad amount for dialing a number. However, if I wanted to make more sales and more money, what would I have to do?

Right, make more dials. That was my first observation from tracking my call-to-close ratios.

But I also realized that I had to face a lot of rejection. Imagine being rejected 285 times out of 300 calls. Discouraging isn't it? Well, I developed an idea to combat this. Knowing I could only obtain five potential prospects out of 100 leads, I changed my strategy and when asked about the franchise opportunity, rather than answer in great detail, I would simply ask a qualifying question and get the suspects "no" quicker. To get more positive responses you have to hear more no's.

If I didn't track my behavior I would have probably given up out of constant rejection.

The other lesson that I learned without me first tracking it related to the time of day that I was calling. After a while I realized that most of the prospects had jobs and had left their home phone number, not their business number. So I had the office get more information when they took the initial call to determine the best time to call and where I was to be calling. Based on this information, I became increasingly productive.

Another important point: many studies reveal that 87 percent of salespeople working the telephone give up after the first attempt. By extrapolation this means that only 13 percent follow up once. Another 10 percent give up after a second call. Only about 3 percent of reps follow up more than once. Which do you think have a higher rate of success?

To get more positive responses, you have to hear more no's. You hear more no's (and more positive responses) by following up every lead and every opportunity. To get more positive responses, you must be tenacious on following up leads. Get the no's out of the way. Being perseverant and persistent is the key and it requires two things: a follow-up system and self-discipline.

The vast majority of reps are not effective at following up simply because they have not developed a system that makes follow-up easy and consistent. Use the tools that make you more efficient—software programs like Tele-Magic, Goldmine, Maximizer, ACT or Outlook. There are also paper-based systems like Franklin Covey or Day Timer. It doesn't matter which system you use, just use one. Don't shove it aside like so many reps do.

When you follow up is just as important as *how* you follow up. Far too many reps will follow up on a letter or fax literally weeks after it has been received. The prospect never remembers the original communication and typically gets the rep to send another letter or whatever. And the cycle begins.

When you send a direct mail piece, follow up two days after its anticipated receipt. If you courier something, follow up within two days. If you send a fax, follow up within one day. If you e-mail, follow up within one day. The collateral material you send should leverage your follow-up call. Timing is absolutely everything. Delaying your follow-up call dilutes the effectiveness of your support documents. If you want more positive responses, make your follow-up calls sooner. By now, you should also realize that you're going to run into voice mail. It's inevitable. In fact, the odds are about 80 percent that you will encounter voice mail in a business-to-business call.

When you do leave a voice mail message, wait three days for a response. If there is no reply, you call again and wait another three days; then again, and again, if necessary. This activity alone puts you into an elite category of sales reps. Remember that 87 percent of reps give up after one call. Your process gives you an immediate competitive advantage and shows persistence without being annoying.

Use your calendar and jot down the follow-up call. If there is no answer, you leave a message, grab the calendar and jot down the date for the next follow-up call and so on. Schedule a specific time to make the follow-up calls. Don't spread them out over the day. Don't pick up the phone on a whim and dial throughout the day. Bunching the calls keeps you focused on the task. You get it done. Also, keep in mind that the time it takes to place a call and leave a voice mail message is insignificant compared to the return. Of course, the composition of your messages for each and every call is equally important. That is where advance preparation, scripting, and trial and error come into play.

This process may feel awkward at first simply because it's new. Feel the discomfort and do it anyway. If you do this for a period of twenty-one days, it will become a habit. The key is to determine the appropriate behaviors and times in which to conduct these behaviors. You then discipline yourself to carry out those behaviors at the appropriate times on a continuing basis. In turn you will up your ROTI—return on time invested—and your bottom line.

Take the time now to customize the tracking chart based on your daily sales behaviors. Then monitor yourself for the next three months to learn your averages, when and where you are getting or not getting results, and how you can improve your call-to-close ratio. I will see you in the next chapter.

Pay Time / No-Pay Time

As salespeople, buyers are the most important component in our jobs. Without them, we have nothing. Because of that, we have to be constantly thinking of buyers in terms of their preferences: *when* do they want to be contacted or visited, *what* are their needs and desires and what can we do to satisfy them, exceed their expectations and add value.

With this in mind, when is the best time for you to be contacting and spending time with prospects and customers? For those selling business to business it is mostly between 9 and 5 on business days. For others, like real estate agents or those in business-to-consumer sales, it is mostly in the evenings and weekends. We have to determine the best time to be in contact with our target market and focus in on those times. I like to refer to this as revenue-generating time or pay time.

Pay time is that time of day when you can be in contact with customers, because that is where your revenue is coming from. So let's define pay-time behaviors as those behaviors that lead us to the accomplishment of our goals or sales quotas. This would include networking, prospecting, telephone, follow up, face-to-face presentations, customer service and so on.

Take a moment and identify the pay-time behaviors that you need to conduct daily to meet your business goals.

Now let's take a look at when these pay-time behaviors should be conducted. As a salesperson, your job is to be proactive wherever possible and reactive less frequently. You know when your customers prefer to be called on. If you are selling business to business, you know that Monday mornings and Friday afternoons are not the best times to be calling on buyers.

Your job is to identify the best times to be in contact with your target market and to carry out pay-time behaviors during those times.

No-pay-time behaviors are the opposite side of pay-time behaviors. No-pay-time behaviors are the supporting tasks we have to attend to as salespeople—filling out call reports, writing letters, sending and replying to e-mail messages, completing and submitting expense reports, attending sales meetings, undertaking training and attending to other corporate demands. None of these will lead to generating more revenue or pay, but they have to be done.

It is these no-pay-time behaviors that you have to control. You still have to do them, but it is *when* you do them that will make the difference. Never use pay time for no-pay-time activities. Keep no-pay-time activities for no-pay time—when you can't be with a prospect or customer or generate any revenue—before or after closing hours, holidays, weekend, etc.

Way too many salespeople manage their time poorly. They use no-pay-time behaviors as excuses to avoid pay-time behavior. Manage your behavior activity during the appropriate pay and no-pay times and you will generate more sales, revenue and goal results.

Combine pay-time with no-pay-time behaviors with the action-oriented behaviors discussed in the earlier chapter on taking action and you will be generating the best ROTI, return on time invested, ever.

Summary

- What are your work expectations and personal desires, keeping in mind that work is a stepping stone to achieving your personal dreams?
- Communicate your work expectations and personal desires to your manager and set win/win objectives.
- Conduct *pay-time* behaviors when buyers are available— prospecting, qualifying, presentations, etc.
- Conduct *no-pay-time* behaviors when buyers are not available—administration, e-mail, internal meetings, training, etc.
- Develop your proactive behaviors to be less reactive.
- Track your behaviors to determine your behavioral ratios—number of calls to appointments, appointments to qualified, qualified to close, etc.
- Complete the exercises: Goal Log, Sales Results Worksheet, Behavior and Tracking Worksheets, Goal Chart, Monthly Monitor Chart

BEHAVIORS TOWARD YOUR BUYERS

The ABCs of Targeting

Prospecting is one of the predominant behaviors required to succeed in sales. Salespeople are required to constantly "fill the funnel" with suspects in order for buyers to come out of the spout of the funnel, thus creating new business. This new business is what keeps you, and everyone else in your organization, employed. Without new business, you will not survive, as existing business diminishes over time due to many factors—economic conditions, competition, relocation, mergers, bankruptcies, etc. New business provides continual growth in revenue, profits and market share.

For many salespeople, prospecting is the most difficult part of their job because it involves cold calls, where one faces more rejection than further down in the funnel. But cold calling has changed a lot over the years. Door-to-door visits and popping in unannounced are no longer effective means of prospecting. Prospecting has become a more sophisticated process.

Prospecting first requires some planning. Let's take a look at the prospecting funnel again and start with your target market.

Is it well defined?

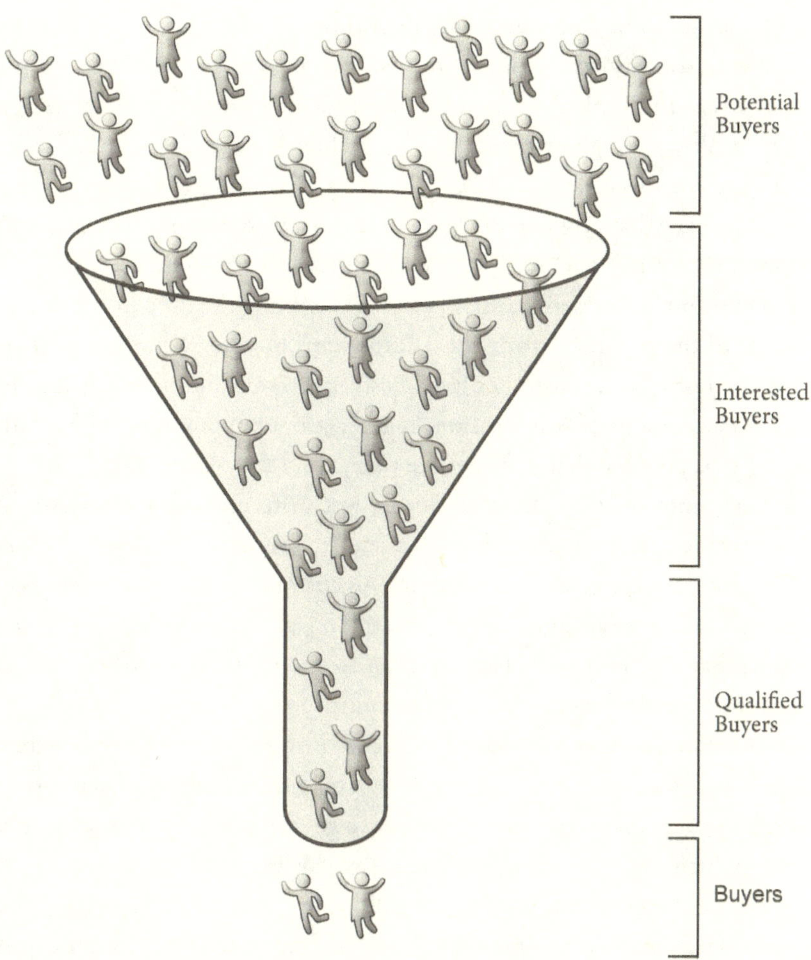

Many organizations and salespeople take the traditional approach and look to the outside to define their markets. You will soon learn that the opposite approach—looking inside—will prove to be more valuable to you and to your future success.

Let's define your target market from the inside out by what you already have: your buyers. If you don't have any buyers and you are starting up, consider whom you would like to have as customers and follow the same process.

First, take a look at your customer base. Identify the common elements between all buyers—industry, size, location, needs, demographics, etc. You will find at least three. They all have a need for your product or service, they have the ability to pay and they have a desire—a desire to purchase from you, usually based on some form of personal relationship. Take the time to identify some of the other common elements and profile your customer base.

Consider these common elements and profile as criteria for your target market.

Next, identify why you are in business. Determine what you want most from your buyers and rank them as an A, B or C. If what you want most is revenue or profit, rank your highest revenue or profit buyers as an "A". Rank the next level as a "B" and the lowest level as a "C". This sort of ranking will identify the big hitters, the 20 percent that give you 80 percent of the revenue or profit. These are your most important buyers, your "A's." At one time they were prospects.

Let's now paint a picture of your "A" buyers—the 20 percent that give you 80 percent of the revenue—**your most important buyers.** What makes them different from the rest of your customer base, besides revenue and profit? Is it a relationship, size, need, demographics, location, market growth, competition? Identify as many elements as possible that differentiate them from the others.

Let's now refer to these common, yet differentiating elements, as criteria. Once these criteria are identified, let's refer to them as Absolute (A) criteria for "A" buyers, as they are also your absolute (A) customers. You absolutely need them to survive. Define the absolute criteria, based on your "A" buyers, as the most important criteria that a suspect must have in order to fit into this category. That criteria must be defined clearly for your "A" buyers and suspects.

Then do the same for your next level of buyers—your "B" or beneficial buyers.

"Why," you ask? Knowing this will help you identify where you should be spending your time prospecting in order to get the best return on your investment in time—which, by the way, is limited and expensive.

Before we move on, answer the following question to yourself: Where do you spend 80 percent of your time—on the 20 percent or the 80 percent of your customer

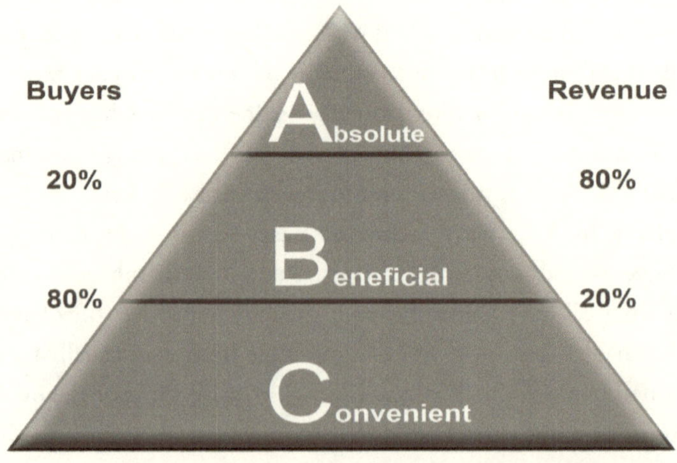

base? Where *should* you be spending your time? Where will you get the best return on your investment in time?

When we take a closer look at these questions, we have to reconsider the traditional approach. Traditionally, salespeople have focused 80 percent of their time on the 20 percent that give them the smallest return on their time investment. In other words, salespeople are not focused on where they can get the best return on time invested. They, too, get caught up in the crisis of the moment and take the easy route as opposed to working on a plan of return on time invested (ROTI).

The ROTI plan in prospecting is to focus your efforts where you will get the best return on your investment in time. To get that return you must know who in your target market will give you the best potential return. Profiling the top 20 percent of your existing business and focusing your efforts on those suspects with the same profile, using the pre-established "A" criteria, will give you a greater return on time invested.

"But wait a minute, Bob," you say. "If I focused all of my attention on the "A's," who will take care of the rest?"

Well the answer is simple: it all depends on how you manage your time and your behavior. There are only so many "A's" out there—20 percent of your target market. Once you have identified them and put a plan of action together and approached them, you then move on to the next level, the "B's" or those suspects that follow the profile and criteria of customers who are not absolutes, but beneficial (B) to your organization. Then there are the "C's" who make up the convenient portion of your customer base. The "C's" are the buyers, or suspects, that provide the smallest contribution to revenue or profit but are convenient to have.

Using the profiles and criteria for each of the A, B and C categories will help you to identify how you should be spending your time. To give you an example, let's look at the airline industry and what makes up a profitable flight. Usually there are three classes of fares: business, economy and seat sale. As you see when you get on the plane, 20 percent of the plane is dedicated toward business class and 80 percent toward economy. Which fare do you think is the most profitable for the airline?

Business class is where 80 percent of the revenue comes from—20 percent of the buyers. They are the absolute buyers as they pay for the flight. Therefore the "A" (absolute) criteria would be based on the profile of business-class travellers. That profile could include being a frequent traveller, a corporate executive or a person who enjoys and can afford the finer side of life. That profile would be used to identify the "A's" in the airline customer base and the suspects in their target market of air travellers.

The next level would be the economy-fare passengers. They pay less, but are greater in volume and usually fill the plane. These are the "B" (beneficial) buyers. They are beneficial to the bottom line.

Then we have the seat sale fares. They fill the plane when economy fare doesn't and are referred to "C" (convenient) buyers. They are convenient to have, but not as beneficial as full-fare economy and certainly not as absolute as the business class traveller.

The same process applies in all industries. Simply identify why you are in business and those clients who contribute the most to that focus. Identify and profile those existing (or potential) buyers who contribute the most to that focus and what criteria it takes to be ranked as the most important—as an A (absolute), followed by the next level B (beneficial) and then C (convenient).

Using the same profile and criteria used on your customer base, identify suspects in your target market using the same A, B and C ranking. Focus your time and efforts in the same manner, mostly on the "A's" (60+ percent) followed by the "B's" (25+ percent) and then the "C's" (15 percent or less). If you follow this planning process for prospecting, your results will improve and your return on time invested will increase dramatically.

This is a small but important part of your "gain strategy." To first rank your suspects, qualify them to prospects and rank those prospects accordingly, based on your pre-identified criteria and on the information you have obtained.

The ABC's Of Targeting

Define **A**bsolute Criteria.

____

____

____

Define **B**eneficial Criteria.

____

____

____

Define **C**onvenient Criteria.

____

____

____

Retain and Regain Strategies

There is another component to consider in the ABC's of Targeting that is not related to prospecting, but deserves a mention. It is related to how you must retain and develop your "A's" while trying to regain past buyers.

You have already identified your most important "A" customers. It is this group of buyers that contributes the most to your business focus. How much time do you spend thanking them for their business, building your relationship with them, staying close and listening to them, going the extra mile for them and contributing to their success? I think you already know the answer. Are you giving them the time they deserve? What are you doing to retain your "A" and "B" buyers?

You have probably heard that it is easier and cheaper to get business out of existing buyers than out of suspects or prospects. This is very true and simple to do. If you want to first retain the business you already have, spend the time with your "A's" and give them the service and attention they need and expect.

Second, your "A" buyers may need more, or something else that you offer, particularly if they are light buyers but meet your "A" criteria. This is where your highest potential for growth exists, but you have to develop the business.

Third, if your buyers like you and the service you are giving them, they will refer *you* to others, or *others* to you. As you know, referrals are easier, more effective and more powerful than cold calls.

Take care of your customers and they will take care of you. Consider this as part of the "retain strategy" that you should take the time to consider and further develop. This is an "A" (absolute) priority.

Now take the time to develop a retain strategy for each level of buyer.

If you did not take the time to develop retain strategies for each level of buyer or did not see this activity as a priority then, you have to consider past buyers and develop a "regain strategy" to gain back those buyers you lost.

If you and your organization do your job well in the first place, you may not need a regain strategy. However, if you do need to regain some past buyers, you must ask yourself, your organization and the client why you lost them, take the blame, apologize, and ask them what it will take to get them back. It is then up to you to get them back or forget them. Just remember that people only tell so many people when they are satisfied, but they tell many more when they are not. As long as it is feasible, do what you have to do to satisfy them to keep them and/or get them back.

On the following pages you will find forms you can use to identify your "A, B and C" present, past and potential buyers along with the strategies identified above. Take the time to complete them.

Present Buyers

Identify Examples of Current Heavy Buyers > **Retain**

Absolute____

Beneficial ____

Convenient ____

Present Buyers

Identify Examples of Current Light Buyers >**Develop**

Absolute____

Beneficial ____

Convenient ____

Past Buyers

Identify Examples of Past Buyers > **Regain**

Absolute____

Beneficial ____

Convenient ____

Potential Buyers

Identify Examples of Potential Buyers > **Gain**

Absolute____

____

Beneficial ____

____

Convenient _______________________________________

____

Gain Strategies

Let's now take a look at your gain strategy. You have defined your target market, the common profile and criteria from your customer base, and ranked each client as an "A" (absolute), a "B" (beneficial) or a "C" (convenient). Your next step is to identify all suspects within your target market, if you can, and rank them similarly as best you can. Then start to work on your gain strategy with a focus on "A" and "B" buyers.

Each organization has a different way of identifying and approaching prospective buyers in their target market. Some organizations use a shotgun approach and go beyond target markets, while others use a more targeted approach, even on a one-to-one basis. Lead generation methods include direct response advertising, direct mail, telemarketing, e-mail, trade shows, public demonstrations and networking. The key is to use the methods that get you the best results in your target market, which is sometimes defined by marketing or the product development group.

Take the time to identify the opportunities you already have to do business with people. These opportunities can come from walk-in traffic, listings in the yellow pages, advertising, your web site, lead generation programs, database management programs, referrals, social functions, etc. List all the avenues that bring potential prospects to your products or services today.

Next, identify opportunities that you can benefit from—opportunities like membership and active participation in associations, networking, trade shows, advertising supplements, sponsorships, partnering, etc. List as many as you can think of that will give you greater opportunities to meet and qualify prospects.

There are many opportunities that you can create to help you increase your opportunities to meet qualified buyers. Gain strategies should include areas where visibility is gained.

You can create press releases based on all kinds of events: new product or service launches, new location, anniversaries, etc. You can write informative or educational articles on your industry, products or services that can be published in targeted magazines with your contact information. You can set up client appreciation, loyalty and referral programs. Get out of the box, brainstorm and list as many creative ways as possible to create new opportunities of meeting potential prospects. Join me back here when you are done.

Now that you have a complete list together, go back and rank the opportunities in order of importance. Which will give you the best return on your investment in time, energy and money? List the most important ones first.

Next, lay out an action plan for the next year. Use this plan as a guide of activities that will get you in front of as many potential prospects as possible. As you complete the performance of each opportunity in the action plan, evaluate each of them for future reference—what worked well, what didn't and what would you do differently next time.

If you are supplied leads, be thankful. All you now have to do, if information on them is provided, is analyze the leads then rank them as A, B or C. If no information is provided, contact the leads and qualify them for prospect status in the relevant priority, or reject them if they do not qualify. Don't try to sell them yet; just qualify them. You will learn more on how to do this in the next section on Competencies. In the meantime, here are some tips on telephone scripting and database management.

Telephone Scripting

You may also need to develop your own leads and that is where a telephone and properly prepared telephone script can do wonders for you. Now when I say script I am not suggesting you read the text when making a call. It is more of a preparation before making the call and knowing what to say.

The first thing you need to do is to define the **objective** of the call, as there are many types of call objectives. Then you need to create your **introduction**: name, business, etc. Where most people fail is in the next statement.

Salespeople tend to talk too much about the organization and/or the products or services they represent. The call is not about you, your organization or the products or services that you offer. It is about the buyer and their needs and if there is an opportunity to do business together or not.

Therefore the next step should be a **unique benefit statement**—a statement that benefits the buyer, not the seller. You have to make a statement that will dictate what is in it for them.

To create your unique benefit statement, answer these two questions:

Why do people buy from you? What is in it for them—the benefits?

My unique benefit statement is as follows: *"We work with organizations like yours to increase the performance of its sales team while contributing to your bottom line."*

Note that this statement says nothing about me, my organization, or the services provided. It only states the benefits the buyer would gain. I also included "like yours" to make them feel comfortable and that they are not alone.

Create your Unique Benefit Statement

____

____

I then follow it up with "**Is this a good time to talk**?" I do this because a telephone call is an interruption and it may, or may not, be a good time to talk, as appealing as my major benefit statement may be. If the answer is no, simply ask, **when would it be a good time**, and call back then.

That covers the opening of the call. The rest is easy and what you hopefully now do: state the purpose of your call; seek permission to ask questions; ask three to five qualifying questions in three to five minutes; determine if they are an A, B or C buyer; if not qualified, thank them for their time and ask for a referral or introduction. If qualified, arrange for a meeting (if that is what you do).

6. Database Management

As you qualify suspects to prospects you have to take the information you gathered and manage it in a database. A database is where you keep all the information you can on every prospect you come across, even after they become a buyer. Maintaining and updating a database is a no-pay-time activity but has all the payback rewards for being disciplined in carrying it out.

There are many programs on the market today that can be used for database management. Select the one that best fits your needs. Whichever program you do use, try to maintain some of the information identified on the following pages.

Industry Information Form

Industry sector: ____________________

Size: ____________________

Rate of growth: ____________________

Trends: ____________________

High-tech changes: ____________________

New product innovations: ____________________

Government regulations: ____________________

Demographics: ____________________

Resources: ____________________

Labor: ____________________

Mergers/Acquisitions: ____________________

Other: ____________________

____

____

____

Sources of Information:

SIC code directories: ____________________

Government sources: ____________________

Industrial guides: ____________________

Industry-specific directories: ____________________

Trade association directories: ____________________

Trade journals: ____________________

Industry experts: ____________________

Internet: ____________________

Other: ____________________

____

____

____

Organization Information Form

Size of organization: ____________________

Structure of organization: ____________________

Rate of growth: ____________________

Products and services: ____________________

Market—local/global: ____________________

Geographic locations: ______________________________

Competition: ______________________________

Culture: ______________________________

Mission statement: ______________________________

Vision: ______________________________

Objectives—short- and long-term: ______________________________

Challenges and opportunities: ______________________________

Needs: ______________________________

Key contacts: ______________________________

Decision maker(s): ______________________________

Purchasing procedures: ______________________________

Other: ______________________________

____

____

____

Sources of Information:

Annual reports: ______________________________

Association reports: ______________________________

Government reports: ______________________________

Internet: ______________________________

News articles: ______________________________

Present customers/suppliers: ______________________________

Other: ______________________________

____

____

____

Buyer Information Form

Identify the areas you feel are valuable for you to know and keep current.

Creation Date: ____________________Last Updated Date: ____________________

Buyer Information:

Name: ____________________

Nickname: ____________________

Job title/position: ____________________

Company name: ____________________

Company address: ____________________

Home address: ____________________

Home phone: ____________________

Business phone/fax/e-mail: ____________________

Birth date: ____________________

Family: ____________________

Hobbies/recreational pursuits: ____________________

Physical conditions, such as back problems, etc.: ____________________

How does buyer like to be contacted?:

(phone, fax, in person, letter, e-mail, etc.) ____________________

Preferred time of day or week for contact: ____________________

Secretary's name: ____________________

Assistant's name: ____________________

Other: ____________________

____

New Buyer

Are there any moral or ethical issues involved in working with this buyer?

____

Does the buyer feel any obligation to you, the company or to the competition?

____

Does the sales proposal you're making require the buyer to change a habit or do something unusual? ____________________

____

Is the buyer overly concerned about the opinion of others? ____________________

____

Are they very self-centered? Are they ethical? ____________________

____

What are the key problems the customer sees? ______________________________

____

What are the priorities of the buyer's management? Any conflicts between buyer and their management: ______________________________________

____

Can you help with these problems? How? __________________________

____

What competitors does the buyer work with? ________________________

____

How close is this relationship? _________________________________

____

What suppliers to the buyer do we know? __________________________

____

Other: ____

____

If you don't want to constantly quiz the customer about details that might seem trivial to them, you could acquire information from other sources, such as their buyers, suppliers, newspapers, trade publications, annual reports, receptionists, assistants and so on. In general, a detailed and well-maintained information system will prove time and again to be an invaluable tool.

You have the right attitude, combining belief with a proactive owner's mentality, and the appropriate behaviors—goals, call-to-close ratios, pay-time, A, B, C targeting, and ROTI . You now need to create your personal marketing plan—a plan that will separate you from all the others, while positioning you as the expert in your market of targeted buyers.

Attracting Buyers—Personal Marketing Plan

A personal marketing plan is different from the gain strategy action plan developed in the last chapter. The gain strategy action plan is mostly based on lead generation through corporate branding and positioning, and is often more of a "push" strategy, pushing your products and services out into the marketplace. In the case of the personal marketing plan, it is based more on a "pull" strategy, attracting buyers to you, as people buy people first.

There are some simple and obvious ways to position yourself for success in your personal marketing program. Keep in mind that the objective behind a personal marketing plan is to attract targeted buyers from being positioned as an expert in your field, while getting the best return on your time invested (ROTI.)

Here are some simple things that you can include in your personal marketing plan:

1. Identify the Associations in Which Your Buyers Are Involved.

A. Purchase a membership. By being a member of the association, you have the opportunity to network and meet potential buyers, in addition to obtaining many other benefits.

B. Become actively involved in a leadership, executive or board role. This increased visibility also gives you more credibility. I have even gone as far as being a founding president of an association chapter. All the members knew who I was and when it came to purchasing services that I offered, to whom would the members turn?

C. Deliver an added-value-content talk. This is the "A" (absolute priority), as it also gives you the best ROTI of all options. Added-value content is always appreciated, but more importantly, the person who is delivering the added-value content is perceived as an expert with credibility because they are standing up in the front of the room and sharing their knowledge, not selling!

Let's pretend selling one-on-one takes thirty minutes. At the end of the thirty minutes, who will be following up or chasing whom? The salesperson will most likely be following up and chasing the buyer. Do you agree?

Speaking to a targeted group of ten, fifty, 100 or more people can also take thirty minutes. At the end of the thirty minutes, who will be following up and chasing whom? A significant percentage of the participants will most likely be following up and chasing the speaker—you. Do you agree?

In the above two examples, which one of the two would give you the best ROTI? One-on-one or one-on-many?

The clear answer: the second one, where you are positioned as an expert with credibility because you are providing added-value content to help the participants save or make money, reduce expenses, increase performance, or whatever buyer benefits your products or services provide, without mentioning or selling them.

Speaking is one of the best personal marketing tools available to you today. CEOs of major corporations understand the importance of speaking to large groups and have become the biggest competitor to professional speakers, as they do not charge a fee, but do position themselves and their organization well in the marketplace.

However, speaking in public is also the #1 fear, followed by death. In other words, people would rather die than speak in public.

Get over it, as it is only a fear. Join a local Toastmasters Club and learn how to become a better communicator. Choose from the many clubs in your city. I am a Toastmaster and I credit Toastmasters International for helping me get where I am today as a professional speaker, trainer and author.

This point leads me to another idea for gaining visibility and credibility with your buyers.

2. Write Articles / Blogs / Tip Sheets

A. E-newsletters. E-newsletters are another inexpensive way to share information with buyers while staying in touch with them on a regular basis. For over fifteen years I have been publishing one, weekly. Each has a personalized greeting, some personal information, a quote and an article that would benefit my buyers/subscribers. Subscribers share it with others, but more importantly, when I meet someone, I add them to the subscribers list within twenty-four hours of meeting them. They receive a personalized auto-responder stating that it was great meeting them and that I want to stay in touch with them via my e-minute, to which they can unsubscribe at any time. Over time the subscriber gets to know me and a relationship is built. In time, they in turn give me business, either directly or through referrals.

B. Magazine / Newspaper Articles. What magazines or newspapers do your buyers read? What would happen if you wrote a value-added-content article and got it published in that magazine or newspaper, along with your photo and contact number? For over fifteen years I have been writing articles and getting them published in a variety of magazines worldwide. I then make photocopies of them and include them in the promo kit that I give buyers, or scan them and include them on my web page.

Every media is looking for information. All you have to do is select the magazine or newspaper and within the first few pages you will find the name and e-mail address of the editor. Send them an e-mail with your article and ask that it be published with your photo and contact details.

Some people get paid to write articles, but I just provide them at no charge. What I get in return is much greater than what they would pay me. Think about this: what would attract the most buyers and give you the most credibility—editorial or an ad?

C. Blogs / Online Articles / Tip Sheets. Similar to the above, select the sites your buyers visit, or simply use your web page for blogs, tips, published articles, etc.

3. Social Responsibility / Charitable Causes

What would happen if you volunteered your time for a major charitable event? Still better, what would happen if you were the public relations person for that event and worked with the media? Would people get to know who you are, and/or whom you represent? Would people buy from you? Would you establish media relationships that could help you in any other way?

4. Press Releases

The media is always in need of newsworthy items. All it takes is writing out a press release following press release guidelines, and circulating it to the media. Sometimes even a call to them gets you coverage, especially if you have an existing relationship with them.

5. Endorsements / Testimonial Letters

Do you have satisfied buyers? Do they tell you how much they enjoy working with you? Do you get it in writing? All you have to do is ask!

Third-party endorsements or testimonial letters are one of the best sales tools available to you. People love to read what other people say about you. It reduces the risk and makes buyers more comfortable buying from you.

When I started my business I created a booklet titled "What people say about Bob." Over the years, following an event, I would thank the buyer for using my services and request their feedback on their letterhead. At least 80 percent of the requests I made were fulfilled, filling my booklet with letters from organizations around the world.

When a buyer asks me why they should use me, I reply with: "*That is a good question. Here is what clients say about me.*" and give them a copy of the booklet. I let my buyers do the selling for me.

6. Referral Reward Programs—Secondary Sales Force

Once you have established and maintained a relationship with a buyer, while providing added value, they in turn can become your secondary sales force by sending you leads, introducing you to other buyers, or by giving you referrals.

Getting introduced or referred to other buyers is a good behavior. Remember, as in discipline, any behavior that gets recognized or rewarded, gets repeated. Establish a referral reward program to recognize and reward buyers so that behavior gets repeated. In no time, you will have a secondary sales force doing all the work for you.

7. Other

What are some other ideas that can increase your credibility and visibility to attract more buyers?

____

With a good personal marketing plan you will be referred and chased through word of mouth as opposed to you having to chase. Everything we discussed so far has cost you nothing other than your time and effort—time and effort you may be presently wasting on traditional techniques that are failing to get you the results you are seeking. If you want to get a better return on your time invested (ROTI), take the time now to outline your personal marketing plan and put it into action!

My personal marketing plan: Actions that can increase my credibility and visibility to attract more buyers?

____

____

____

____

Summary

- Eighty percent of your business comes from 20 percent of your buyers—the 80/20 rule. Prioritize your buyers and prospects accordingly: A, B, C.
- Determine the Absolute (A), Beneficial (B) and Convenient (C) criteria for each level of buyer and prospect.
- Develop Retain, Regain and Gain strategies to maintain and increase your buyer base.
- Create a telephone script, using a unique benefit statement, with permission to talk now and ask questions.
- Create a database to maintain buyer information and keep it up to date at all times.
- Create a personal marketing plan that will give you the credibility and visibility to attract targeted buyers.

Review and Daily Disciplines for Behavior: Your Bottom Line

In this category on behavior you learned first about your behavior toward yourself, as this is the driver for all other behaviors.

You learned why you go to work, and how work is a stepping stone to getting you where you want to go. You learned how to set SMART goals that are Specific,

Measurable, Attainable, Relevant and Trackable to a Timetable. You learned how to complete each component of a goal log and completed additional goal logs for each of your main category goals. Finally, you made a commitment to yourself to follow through and do what you have to do while learning that nothing happens without taking action. You were also provided with some valuable support tools: the Soar Chart and the Monthly Monitor Chart.

You then moved into behavior toward your organization and defined and communicated your work expectations and personal desires to your manager and set win/win objectives.

You completed goal logs for each of your top three organizational goals, using the support of your Sales Results, Soar and Monthly Monitor Charts.

You learned how to track your behaviors to determine your behavioral call-to-close ratios—the number of calls to appointments, appointments to qualified, qualified to close, etc.

You learned about when to conduct *pay-time* behaviors and when to conduct *no-pay-time* behaviors and reviewed your proactive Behaviors to be less reactive.

We looked at your behavior toward buyers, where you learned that 80 percent of your business comes from 20 percent of your buyers—the 80/20 rule. You learned how to Prioritize your buyers accordingly—A, B and C—and identified the criteria for each level of buyer.

You developed Retain, Regain and Gain strategies to maintain and increase your buyer base; and, finally, you created a personal marketing plan that will give you the credibility and visibility to attract targeted buyers.

You learned about telephone scripting and the kind of information you need to maintain.

You learned a lot. All that is left to do is for you to reflect on all of the learning you received. It is now time to write out the daily disciplines you want to instil in your life and then do what you have to do. Remember that any behavior that gets recognized or rewarded gets repeated, so include them as well.

Daily Disciplines: Behavior - Your Bottom Line

What did you learn?

____

____

____

____

____

It is now time to set those ***daily disciplines and do what you have to do.*** Remember that any behavior that gets recognized or rewarded gets repeated.

1. What daily disciplines do you want to apply for yourself?

___

___

___

What will your reward be for doing what you say you will do?

___

___

___

2. What daily disciplines do you want to apply toward your Organization?

___

___

___

What will your reward be for doing what you say you will do?

___

___

___

3. What daily disciplines do you want to apply toward buyers?

___

___

___

What will your reward be for doing what you say you will do?

___

___

___

Reminder: review these disciplines daily for the next twenty-one consecutive days, or using the Monthly Monitor Chart for twenty-five out of thirty-one days and you will make these disciplines effective habits.

COMPETENCIES—THE "BUYER FOCUSED" VELOCITY SELLING SYSTEM, PART 1

The Four Steps on How Buyers Buy

The Four Universal Needs of Buyers

The Three Competencies You Need to Master First

1. Buyer Focused
2. Buyer Engagement
    A. Asking Questions
    B. Listening Skills
3. Buyer Empowerment

Equipped with a fantastic attitude and appropriate goal-driven behaviors, it is now time to add the **"C"** that stands for competencies. You need the competencies of your profession, as a lawyer or doctor needs them for theirs. You know your target and where to reach them. You now need to learn the "Buyer Focused" Velocity Selling System in order to engage and empower buyers to buy.

Where can you develop your competencies? Almost anywhere. As salespeople we could develop our competencies by reading books, by in-class or online virtual training, by on-the-job training or activities, by being coached, or through trial and error. We could join professional sales associations, and, in some countries, we can even become certified as sales professionals.

In this category we are going to discuss the competencies required to be a success in sales when you are face to face with a prospective buyer, having a conversation over the telephone, online or communicating via e-mail. The competencies will also be outlined in the form of a process, a step-by-step system. This process has been tried and proven internationally for varied goods and services, in all kinds of industries.

Although salespeople need many competencies, the essential ones boil down to human interaction, communication and relationship building. Gone are the traditional days of the slick, hit-and-run "feature and benefit" dumps (overwhelming listeners with all the attractive features of the product and how it will benefit them). Why? Because every buyer has been educated by us in the past and they have responded by creating their own system to maintain control over salespeople.

Over time, buyers were appalled by our high-pressure tactics, sleazy sales gimmicks and manipulative closing techniques. Consequently, they gained more control as information became easier to gather and to evaluate via the internet.

Buyers today can purchase whatever they want, whenever they want, without a salesperson confronting them and wasting their time. The #1 buyer complaint about salespeople, and I quote, is that "they waste my time."

Traditionally, salespeople have been taught a lot of sales techniques and tactics. Most of these work for a while. However, over the years we have "trained" buyers on these techniques and tactics, as buyers see more salespeople in a day than salespeople see buyers. Buyers know that salespeople have received sales training and when they meet with us, they usually see the same techniques and tactics being applied. As a result, salespeople have taught buyers everything they know and buyers have developed a process to counteract the actions of salespeople.

The worst part is, salespeople don't even realize they have lost control, leaving the buyer in control of the interaction, when salespeople themselves should always remain in control of the sales process. It is the salesperson's responsibility to qualify the buyers. However, over the years the buyers have taken control and end up qualifying the salespeople and their products and services. Think about it. How do prospects respond to most of your methods and techniques? Who is rejecting whom?

Who should be rejecting whom? Are you in control of the sales process, or do you just "think" you are?

The time has come. Now, it is a clear-cut case of being professional and following a non-traditional proven sales results system. Do the opposite of what you may have been trained to do—that is if we want to be different than most salespeople out there. The difference is that you will have your prospects buy *from* you, rather than being sold something *by* you.

The "Buyer Focused" Velocity Selling System will help you to establish rapport and build trust, to communicate effectively and to develop and maintain lasting relationships. It is a system that will put you in control and allow you to quickly qualify prospects on several levels, to determine next steps, to prescribe solutions, to let the buyer buy, all while retaining and developing the relationship for more business, referrals and introductions.

Without a sales results system, salespeople are working on a hit-and- miss basis, wasting time and not getting the results they could be getting. They become a slave to the buyer's system. A professionally trained salesperson following a sales results system is a very powerful tool in any organization. Remember, without sales, there are no transactions. No transactions translates into no revenue. Without revenue, jobs and organizations don't exist, no matter how good the product or service.

So, let's first review some important prerequisites to the System, Part 1.

THE FOUR STEPS ON HOW BUYERS BUY

To better understand the "Buyer Focused" Velocity Selling System, we need to first take a look at how buyers buy and why they react to salespeople like they do.

You are a consumer or a buyer and you meet up with a salesperson, or an actual salesperson with another title that he or she is hiding behind. What is your initial reaction? Do you tell them you are so happy to see them because you have money to spend today on their particular product or service? No, I don't think so.

Your first reaction, as a buyer, may be to establish control by asking the salesperson some questions about their products or services and not answering too many of their questions. Or you may ignore them or tell them you are just looking? If this is what you are used to doing as a consumer or buyer, you are just like most consumers and professional buyers out there. Let me share a typical example with you.

Pretend for a moment that you wanted to buy an appliance or a piece of furniture for your home. You walk into a furniture store and a salesperson comes up to you and says what? Yes—"Can I help you." This seems to be the standard line everywhere. What is your response? "No, I am just looking."

Now, why did you answer like that? You knew what you were looking for and you know the salesperson can help you.

Why do you think consumers and buyers act this way? Is it because we are bad people and we want to take advantage of salespeople? Or, is it because we don't trust salespeople and they need to earn that trust first? Is it also fair to say that it is ok to mislead a salesperson, because consumers know salespeople may mislead them?

As a consumer you feel you are still going to get to heaven, as it is normal to lie to salespeople because you know they will lie to you.

This is the first step in the buyer's system. The buyer will initially always mislead a salesperson. It is up to the salesperson to gain the buyer's trust first.

Quite often in my training sessions I play a game called Password. I get the participants to pretend they are consumers, or the general public, and have absolutely nothing to do with sales. I then place the word "salesperson" on the flip chart and ask them what words come to mind. Even with a very professional sales class I get the same answers. "What sort of words, or thoughts, come to your mind?"

I always hope that some of those words and thoughts will be positive and professional. Unfortunately, most of the words are not. Try playing the game with others and see what they say.

Yes, "sales" is regarded as the lowest form of profession there is by the general public. Yet I believe that the profession of sales is the greatest profession of all. The world revolves around sales. Remember, without a buyer and a transaction, there is no revenue and no organization can survive no matter how great its products or services.

Back to the Password game. I also get a lot of words like "confident," "helpful," "knowledgeable," "resourceful," "professional," "courteous," "polite," etc. Now that is more like it, you say? Well, with the bad comes the good. There are many very good salespeople out there and they do set themselves apart and are very successful because of what they are doing.

Most salespeople are on time for scheduled meetings and do provide solutions within your budget and time constraints. In addition, by following the "Buyer Focused" Velocity Selling System, salespeople will learn how to quickly gain trust, eliminate surprises, uncover buying opportunities and either provide a solution within the prospect's budget and time constraints or tell the prospect, "I'm sorry, I can't help you." This makes the salesperson even more professional, staying in control and still building a relationship while acquiring referrals and introductions.

One of the biggest problems in sales is that salespeople are so knowledgeable about their organization's products and/or services that they feel they have to give that information away, even if the buyer doesn't ask for it. I like to refer to this as free consulting. For some reason salespeople feel the more information they give the more sales they will get. Buyers like this about salespeople. It gives them a chance to stay in control. Think about it. Do you freely share your knowledge with the prospect?

Let's face it, salespeople are by far the most knowledgeable people in every organization. They know the products and services well, their unique advantages and disadvantages, features and benefits, pricing, margins and discounts, production and delivery, organizational structure, competition, market and company strengths, weaknesses, threats and opportunities, mission, vision, etc. Salespeople deserved to be recognized for this, but at the same time they need to learn to be discreet, or better still, to shut up.

I provide consulting and coaching services to sales and sales management within many organizations. Where would my business be in three months if I were to give away everything I knew for free? I would be down the hole in no time and you will be too if you don't put a cap on the information you are giving away.

Why do you think buyers want to know everything you know? Right, so they can make an informed decision. But is it not also because they want to compare you to the competition? They want to know everything you know and they don't want to pay for it. I refer to this as free consulting. Think about it, what is the result of giving your expertise to the buyer?

Free consulting is the second step in the buyer's system. Buyers will use their questioning techniques to take control of the process. They will ask you tons of questions to which you normally have to hesitate before answering. You feel that they are legitimate questions and so you respond.

They is nothing wrong with that, is there? Yes, there is. The person answering the questions may think they are in control, but they are not. It is your job as a salesperson to qualify the buyer, not have the buyer qualifying you. Your job is to ask questions, not give information away, particularly for free.

The funny part is most salespeople have not learned this yet. They give away tons of information and then, what sort of an answer do they generally get from the buyer? "Thank you, I want to buy!" No, I don't think so. How about, "Thank you for all of the information; let me get back to you." Or, "I need to think it over; I'll get back to you." Or, "I will discuss it with the others and get back to you."

You have heard all of these lines before, haven't you? What happens? What do they really mean without saying it? Is it fair to say the buyer is misleading us again? This is step three in the buyer's system. They really mean to say "No, I am not interested," but they don't want to hurt your feelings, or they figure they could never get rid of you if they did say no because you have been trained to only go for a yes. Don't worry; I will teach you the opposite—how to go for a no.

Now the buyer has misled us, gathered all the information they need for free and misleads us again. As a salesperson you end up with the impression that you have a sale coming. However, it is really only a "hope-a"— I hope I got a sale.

Because you have been well trained, you have gotten all of the buyer's contact information and you decide to follow up with them. What usually happens? Do they take your call? Do they return your voice or e-mail messages? If so, great! You have managed to gain some trust and started to develop a relationship. If not, you have fallen into the buyer's system once again.

Hiding is the fourth step of the buyer's system. They don't return your calls or e-mail messages. Why? Maybe because they found a better deal, a better product or service, or maybe a better salesperson—one who asked questions, took the time to show he or she cared by listening to the buyer's needs while helping the buyer buy. You can tell and sell or you can do the opposite—ask and let them buy. Keep doing what you have always done and you will always get what you have gotten.

The four-step process in Part 2 of Competencies: the "Buyer Focused" Velocity Selling System will reveal the opposite approach to you, allowing you to gain and stay in control so that you can qualify the prospect first, before providing any solutions or free consulting.

However you must first learn the universal needs of buyers and how to engage and empower buyers to buy.

Summary

- The salesperson is misled. "No need, just looking."
- Buyers will try to get as much information from the salesperson as possible—free consulting— so they can shop and compare price.
- The salesperson will be misled again. "Let me think it over" or "I'll get back to you."
- When you follow up with the buyer, they hide and don't return phone calls or e-mail messages.

UNIVERSAL NEEDS OF BUYERS

All buyers have needs and there are four universal needs in particular that salespeople need to work on to be buyer focused.

1. The need to be understood.

The first need is that buyers have a need to be understood. That means you must listen to them and question them to better understand them. The problem many salespeople have is that they don't listen and, worst yet, they don't question the answers they receive to get even more information. There is more to come on this in the Asking Questions section.

As a buyer, do you like it when a salesperson takes the time to understand you? If so, how does the salesperson begin to understand you, and if he is sincere, how does it make you feel? In your experience, how often are you treated this way at home, at work and in the marketplace?

What are some of the things you can do to make your buyer feel they are being understood?

____

2. The need to feel welcomed.

The second universal need is that buyers need to feel welcomed. How do you welcome people that come and visit you at home? Do you welcome buyers the same way, even in their own premises?

As a buyer, do you like that a salesperson is welcoming? If so, how does the salesperson welcome you and how does it make you feel? In your experience, how often are you treated this way at home, at work and in the marketplace?

What are some of the things you can do to make your buyer feel welcomed?

---

3 The need to feel important.

Buyers have the need to feel important. How important do you make them feel in your presence? Using their name, asking questions and taking notes is one way to do that.

As a buyer, do you like it when a salesperson takes the time to make you feel important? If so, how does the salesperson go about making you feel important and how does it make you feel? In your experience, how often are you treated this way at home, at work and in the marketplace?

What are some of the things you can do to make your buyer feel important?

---

4. The need to feel comfortable.

Buyers also have the need to feel comfortable. How can you make them more comfortable? There are many ways from offering a seat or water to eliminating surprises.

As a buyer, do you like it when a salesperson takes the time to make you feel comfortable? If so, how does the salesperson go about making you feel comfortable, and how does it make you feel? In your experience, how often are you treated this way at home, at work and in the marketplace?

What are some of the things you can do to make your buyer feel comfortable?

The following sections will help you with all of these needs.

Summary—Universal Needs of Buyers

1. The need to be understood
2. The need to feel welcomed.
3. The need to feel important.
4. The need to feel comfortable.

THE THREE COMPETENCIES YOU NEED TO MASTER FIRST

Buyer Focused

The world revolves around sales. Buyers are everywhere. What are you doing to help them buy?

In order to succeed in sales you need to do the opposite of selling. You need to attract, engage and empower buyers to buy.

The sales process has to be transformed to a no-pressure exchange where "getting to the truth" and building a relationship is the goal.

It becomes more important to bring in the right buyers for the right reasons instead of simply making a sales pitch or even a sale.

If you truly want to be the problem-solver and be sincere, then do away with the traditional or consultative approach with today's new economy of buyers.

Most organizations today are aware that the economy has brought on a shift from selling during the boom times to attracting, engaging and empowering the new economy of buyers to buy.

This is where the change has to begin: to change the focus from you, your organization, its products and/or services, to the buyer. It is no longer about what you can do for the buyer. In this new economy of buyers it is all about the buyer and what they can do for you.

When you put your focus on the buyer and their universal needs instead of your needs, you start the transformation. You gain more respect and trust, more relationships, shorter sales cycles, increased margins and revenues, and a better bottom line.

What can you do to help buyers buy?

Buyer Engagement

All buyers want to be engaged. After all, it is all about them and their needs, desires, budget, etc. This is where communication skills—asking questions and listening attentively, come into play.

In order to master the Velocity Selling System, a salesperson must discard old selling habits in exchange for new sales behaviors. A new approach to buying and selling requires effort and perseverance but in no time you will master the system. The overall sales cycle will be shortened, your sales will increase and you will "up your bottom line."

You cannot become competent in the Velocity Selling System unless you already have a solid foundation and strong supporting walls on which you can rely.

For example, it is a universal requirement to understand the buyer. A salesperson must be competent at asking questions and listening intently to the answers.

Competency takes practice, which is a progressive daily behavior. Competency is a learned behavior. Behavior is a habit and ultimately, the particular way you do things. Before you can become competent at asking questions and listening attentively, you must practice asking questions and listening attentively as a progressive daily behavior.

But first, you must have the desire to want to engage and understand buyers. Do you have that desire?

If so, you can do this by asking significant questions and listening intently. This is an encouraging attitude.

We have worked on the attitudes and behaviors required to succeed. Now you must become competent at engaging buyers by asking questions and listening attentively.

So, let's get started on one of the most important sections, **Asking Questions**.

Asking Questions

The most important communication skills required in the Velocity Selling System are asking questions and listening to the answers, as they contribute directly to qualifying buyers and building relationships. In these sections on Buyer Engagement, you will learn how to ask more effective questions and how to apply effective listening. Once you have mastered these two skills you will be in a better position to complete the four-step "Buyer Focused" Velocity Selling System in part 2.

Questions contribute to a self-discovery process, which is a buying process. The salesperson asks the buyer questions that lead the buyer to discover their own needs and solutions within their budget and decision-making process. Buyers must come up with the answers themselves. You can't tell them, as they must own those answers. You just have to know what questions need to be asked in order to get the answers you are seeking.

Let's first understand why you should be asking questions. By asking questions you not only learn a lot, but you also uncover needs and make the other person feel important, helping to build a lasting relationship. While there are millions of reasons for asking questions, there is one that is most important for salespeople to understand and to master.

As you know, it is the salesperson's responsibility to qualify buyers, yet it is the buyer who qualifies the salesperson most of the time. This is witnessed by the buyer asking the salesperson questions, and the salesperson answering those questions while ending up in step 2 of the buyer's system, giving free consulting.

Yet it is the salesperson's responsibility to gather information, not give it away. It is when salespeople start to give information away—free consulting—that they start to lose control.

The one main reason for salespeople to ask questions is to maintain control of the sales process: to build rapport and to gather information to determine whether the buyer is qualified for the solutions you provide and then to make a decision to proceed or to abort. When a salesperson is not in control of the process, they have fallen into the buyer's system.

So, how do you get information and stay in control of the sales process? You ask questions. It is always the person asking the questions who is in complete control. The person who is answering the questions thinks they are in control, but in reality they are not. It is the salesperson's responsibility to be in control of the process, but it is the buyer who should think he or she is in control.

We created a rule here for you to stay in control of the sales process. It is really the 80/20 rule, but to distinguish it from the 80/20 rule, we refer to this rule as the **70/30 rule**. Seventy percent of the time you should be listening. Thirty percent of the time you should be asking questions. Added up, the two equal 100 percent. In other words, there is no room for talking in the Velocity Selling System until you get to step 3—Prescribing Solutions.

Take a moment and highlight why we ask questions and the 70/30 rule.

The first step of the Velocity Selling System is to build rapport and gain the buyer's trust. We will discuss this in detail in the upcoming chapters, but for now, let's keep our focus on questioning techniques. One of the best ways to build rapport is to ask open-ended questions about the buyer that will get the buyer to open up and start talking.

Your job is to establish rapport, to get the buyer talking, keep them talking and then direct them with questions that will lead them to where you want to go, while you gather more information and facts. But first, where is it that you want to go; what is your objective? You need to answer this question before you proceed.

Your objective should not be to make a sale, but to establish a relationship and to qualify the buyer to determine if there is an opportunity to do business, or not. Making a sale is secondary. This attitude alone will make the difference in your approach. Obviously, if the buyer is not qualified, you cannot help him, and there is no need to waste any more of your time. However, because you have established a relationship, they may be in a position to refer you to others who are qualified.

> *Sales is a people business and it is all about relationships. The more relationships you have, the bigger your network will be. The bigger your network, the bigger your Net Worth.*
>
> **—Bob Urichuck**

So before we go any further, let's understand the types of questions that can be used and why. Let's start with how you can use open-ended questions to your advantage.

Typically, **open-ended questions** begin with what, how, who, why and where. They get buyers to open up and feel a greater sense of participation in an interview, engaging them while giving the discussion a more conversational tone. Open-ended questions encourage a prospective buyer to respond at length, providing you with information critical to the sale. Not only useful as fact-finding, these questions uncover underlying attitudes, opinions and feelings. They help buyers clarify their thinking, leading them to identify and verbalize their own needs, needs that you can then paraphrase.

Open-Ended Questions

Typically, open-ended questions begin with what, how, who, why and where.

Purposes:

1. To allow people to feel a greater sense of participation in an interview.
2. To give the discussion a more conversational tone.
3. To encourage a prospective buyer to respond at length, providing you with information that is critical to the sale.
4. To uncover underlying attitudes, opinions and feelings as well as find facts.
5. To help prospective buyers clarify their thinking.
6. To help prospective buyers to identify and verbalize their own needs.
7. To provide you with information that you may in turn paraphrase.

Sample Rapport-Building Questions

What kind of movies do you enjoy?
What music do you prefer?
Who is your favorite artist / group?
What kind of car do you drive?
How do you like it?
How old are your children?
What are their names?
Where are you going on your vacation?
Tell me about your…
What type of work do you do?
How long have you been doing that?
What do you enjoy most about it?
What sports interest you?

Other Examples of Open-Ended Questions:

1. How does this affect your business?
2. What is it you like about brand X?
3. Why is that important to you?
4. Why do you say that?

Take the time to generate open-ended questions that will be useful in your sales interview, starting with the first question you would use when you first meet up with a prospective buyer. This is a very important exercise and it is recommended that you work on establishing open-ended questions before moving on to directing questions.

You can always tell when you have established rapport just by noticing how much the buyer starts to open up to you. It is as if they will never stop talking. Of course that is your job, to establish rapport, to get the buyer talking, keep them talking and direct them with questions that will lead them to where you want to go, while you gather more information and facts. But first, where is it that you want to go; what is your objective? You need to answer this question before you proceed.

Next we have Directing Questions

Occasionally, you need to point your buyer in a particular direction—a direction that will provide you with new information in areas of specific interest.

The purpose of asking directing questions is to stimulate thinking in new directions, to cause the buyer to evaluate the consequences of not acting, or to force a reply that you wish to hear or to force a choice in order to help you guide the discussion in the right direction.

Questions that perform these functions for you are also referred to as **leading questions**. Note that leading questions can either open up the discussion or focus in on the discussion, depending on your purpose at a specific point in time.

Directing Questions

Purposes:

1. To stimulate thinking in new directions
2. To cause the buyer to evaluate the consequences of not acting.
3. To force a reply that you wish to hear.
4. To force a choice in order to help you guide the discussion in the right direction.

Examples:

What would happen if...?

1. What would happen if you didn't...?
2. So, you think it would be wise to...?
3. Do you prefer...?

Then take the time to generate some directing questions that will be useful in your sales interview.

Fact-Finding and Closed-Ended Questions are used when you need brief short, to-the-point answers to gather facts, "break the ice" and set the "ground rules." Fact-finding and closed-ended questions can also be used to attract the attention of someone unwilling to talk or to re-focus the conversation, to check for his/her degree of understanding or interest, or to confirm an agreement.

Fact-Finding and Closed-Ended Questions

When you need short, to-the-point answers.

Purposes:

1. To gather facts.
2. To "break the ice" and set the "ground rules."
3. To attract the attention of someone unwilling to talk or to re-focus the conversation.
4. To check for degree of understanding or interest.
5. To confirm an agreement.

Examples of yes or no, closed-ended questions

1. Would this plan meet your needs?
2. Do you currently buy from more than one supplier?

Examples of fact-finding closed-ended questions

1. How many people do you employ?
2. What brand of product are you currently using?

Take the time to generate some fact-finding and closed-ended questions that will be useful in your sales interview.

Using the questions you wrote out will help you be more prepared for when you contact or meet a prospective buyer. As you move forward, you should create a list of questions that will uncover potential problems, pains or pleasures for which you have solutions.

First let's understand why people buy. People buy because they want to satisfy a need. However, many people think that the process of buying is intellectual and requires the salesperson to provide features and benefits. Well, folks, once again, it is the opposite that is true. People don't buy for intellectual reasons; they buy for emotional reasons—to solve a pain or to gain a pleasure. They justify their purchase intellectually. And yes, there is a role for features and benefits, but it comes later in the process.

In order to be successful in our communications we must first understand our buyers, as that is one of their universal needs—to be understood. We do this by asking questions and listening. Only in this way can we qualify our prospective buyers and determine if there is a need, and if we can provide a solution to that need, or not. Only after this point can we communicate our position.

In the second step of the "Buyer Focused" Velocity Selling System–Qualifying Buyer Opportunities, you will learn how you need to identify three to five problems, pains or pleasures, by asking a lot of questions. The more pains or pleasures identified, the higher the likelihood of making a sale. You have heard it said before: "No pain, no gain."

Here is a simple exercise for you. Start by first listing all the solutions that you provide. Then list the potential problems, pains or pleasures that each solution solves. Then develop questions that will help uncover some of those problems, pains or pleasure.

Turning Telling into Asking Exercise

- Solutions that my products and services provide are:
- The pain and / or pleasures these solutions solve are:
- The questions I need to ask to uncover the pain and/or pleasures for which we have solutions are:

Solutions	Pain/ Pleasure solved	Questions to uncover the Pain/ Pleasures for which you have solutions

As you proceed to ask questions, you can also expect the buyer to be asking you questions. This is where you can lose control. You lose control by answering the questions, and even more if you get into a lot of details. Your job is to introduce yourself, state your name and company and your unique benefit statement on how you help organizations like theirs in your specific industry. But before you can tell them anything more, you need to know a lot about them. How you do this will be discussed in greater detail in the second step of the "Buyer Focused" Velocity Selling System: Setting Parameters. For now, let me just share with you how to maintain control by using some internationally proven techniques. I would suggest that you highlight the following techniques, as they are so important for you to master.

The first technique is Respect-Repeat-Reverse

When asked a question, you need not respond, as you may have always done. When you are asked a question, first take the time to respect the question. That is done by giving the buyer a compliment—something along the lines of, "That is a great question, John." Then you need to repeat the question and reverse it back to the prospective buyer, i.e. "Would that be important to you and why?" By doing this you obtain additional information, clarity and stay in control.

Reversing helps you in several ways. It keeps the prospect talking, allowing you to gather more information, which leads to more questions. Reversing also shifts the focus from you to the buyer, where it belongs. Questions show you are interested in the buyer; it makes them feel important and understood, while building rapport and supporting your credibility.

Alternatively you can provide a brief Answer but you must always End with a Question.

Another way of staying in control when asked a question is to again respect the question by complimenting the prospect and providing a brief answer, but to end with a question back to the buyer. If you don't, you are giving the prospect another chance to question you and you will eventually lose control and end up in the buyer's system.

For example

"Tell me about your business, Bob."

"Thanks for asking, John. There is a lot that I can tell you. Is there something in particular that you would like to know?"

Or

"Thanks for asking, John. We work with organizations like yours to improve the performance of its salespeople while contributing to your bottom line. Would that be of interest to you, John?"

Yes!

"What are some of the performance issues that you are facing, John?"

A word of caution. **If you are asked the same question twice, answer it.** Don't antagonize the buyer. Ask another question and move on. It is rare that a prospect would ask the same question twice.

Questions can also be **used to handle objections**. When the buyer presents an objection to you, respect it and reverse it, turning it back to them. Quite often I will get an objection that I am too expensive. I always say, "That is an interesting observation; why do you think I am so expensive?" I always get an answer on why I am and—you know what—their answer doesn't really matter to me, so long as it is **their answer and not mine**. They need to own the answer to their objection. You should never have to justify your prices or fees, your product, your service, organization or what you do for a living. Make it a practice to stop justifying and start reversing the pressure to where it belongs—back to the buyer.

Earlier you learned **the 70/30 rule.** It is very important for you to keep the prospect talking. If they are not talking, you end up talking and that is very dangerous. The 70/30 rule applies here as it does elsewhere. Your job is to get the prospect talking by asking questions 30 percent of the time so that you are listening 70 percent of the time.

There is another important rule that you need to be made aware of: **the Rule of 3+**

The best way to keep the buyer talking, while getting to the real problem or desired pleasure, is by asking questions, listening to the answer then questioning that answer. The more you do this, the closer you will get to the real issue, while helping the buyer discover his/her need on their own.

Most salespeople have a problem doing this, because when you ask a question, you are not listening to the answer, you are too busy thinking of the next question to ask. Stop doing that. The technique is simple. Listen to the answer and question the answer. Don't get derailed by thinking of another question and moving away from the opportunity of going deep.

Remember to always question the answers three to five levels deep to get more clarity, information and to the truth. Don't ever just accept the first answer to a question.

For example, let me ask you a question, "Why do you go to work?" You probably answered, "To make money." Now question the answer, "Make money to do what?" Question the answer, listen to the answer, question the answer, listen to the answer and you will soon discover why you really go to work. You will realize that you go to work for your personal reasons—by working you are taking steps toward the realization of a personal dream. Realize that and you will be more motivated in going to work.

This is a great technique once mastered.

The next technique is Strip Line

Simple statements like "That's interesting; tell me more" can keep the buyer talking. The strip-line technique is particularly useful when the prospect is showing interest in your product or service during the prescription phase. Rather than going for a trial close, get them to tell you why they are interested or what it is that made them feel like they do. Empower them with the opportunity to sell themselves.

Another technique to get and keep the buyer talking, and more importantly, to get commitment, is the "**let's-pretend**" technique. The let's-pretend technique is simply asking in a way that leads to a response and a commitment from the buyer. As a rule, you should never do something for a buyer unless you know what will happen next. You need to be constantly seeking a clear future.

The let's-pretend technique can be used in many ways: a demo, a visit, a test drive, a presentation, etc. It should be always be used to gain a commitment from the buyer as to what will happen next? If there is no commitment as to what will happen next, you are probably wasting your time.

Let's pretend example

Salesperson: "As soon as I hang up I will mail that information to you. When would you expect to receive it?"

Buyer: "By Wednesday."

Salesperson: "Let's pretend it is Wednesday and that information is now in front of you, what would happen next?"

Buyer: "I would review it and make probably make a decision."

Salesperson: "Ok, whether you are interested, or not, can I at least get the professional courtesy of a reply."

Buyer: "Yes"

Salesperson: "When can I expect to hear back from you?"

Buyer: "On Thursday."

Salesperson: "Great. If I do not hear back from you on Thursday, can I follow up with you on Friday?"

Buyer: "Yes."

Salesperson: "Is there anything in particular that you would like me to say when I call?"

Buyer: "Just mention the brochure and price list you sent me."

Salesperson: "Thank you for your request and I look forward to hearing back from you Thursday."

Did the salesperson get a commitment? Yes, the buyer will call him on Thursday.

Will the buyer call him on Thursday? Probably not.

Did the salesperson get permission to follow up? Yes.

When the salesperson follows up as agreed, how does that make the buyer feel?

Guilty, as charged.

When someone feels guilty, because they did not do what they said they were going to do, what usually happens?

The next helpful technique is what I refer to as the Magic Wand

As you know, a magic wand can provide you with anything you desire. It makes the impossible possible and is used with a buyer to seek out clarity in their needs or desires.

For example, "If you had a magic wand, and nothing was impossible, what would be the ideal solution you would wish for?"

Alternatively, "Let's pretend that nothing was impossible and that you could have a solution to that problem; what sort of a solution do you feel would work best for you?"

A magic wand takes down barriers and gets the buyer dreaming. Your job is to note their desires and then ask, "Which one or two of these desires are the most important out of the six I have listed?" If you can satisfy them, or at least their top desires, they will buy.

You are on page 7 and I am on page 2

What if you are asked a question about price or a solution early in the cycle before you have the information you need to gather to qualify them? Mention that you will give them an answer to that question soon but you need to gather more information first. For example, *"You are on page 7 and I am only on page 2; there is more information that I need to know before I can answer that question properly."* If they insist on the price, reveal your highest price, as it is easier to come down in price than it is to raise it.

Wishy-washy words

When communicating with a buyer you will sometimes get wishy-washy answers back. If you are not sure what they mean, question them. You will always get improved clarity by asking additional questions. Quite often I hear answers like "*maybe*," "*leave it with me*," or "*I'll think it over and get back to you.*" I always question these answers because they are not clear to me.

For example, *"When you say maybe, what does that mean?"* or "*When you say you will think it over and get back to me, what exactly will you be thinking over and when can I expect to hear back from you?"* If I don't have clear answers, I have nothing but a hope of a sale. I always make it a point to get a clear response so I know exactly where I stand.

By asking questions, you will remain in control. Questions will help you gain a lot more information. Questions will handle objections and concerns. Questions show that you care and that you are interested and willing to learn more. Questions help in self-discovery and it is the self-discovery process that gets people to buy, because they own the answers. Master the act of questioning and staying in control of the sales process. But make sure you listen to what the answers are, and question those answers.

What are some wishy-washy words that you get and how can you handle them?

Here are some examples:

"I'll get back to you."

When?

"Maybe."

Meaning?

"I'll think about it."

Sure, I can understand that. Many of my buyers like to think about their purchases. What is it you would like to think about?

"I need to check with my spouse."

I can appreciate that. I am married too and I check with my spouse when making a major purchase. What concerns do you think she may have?

"It's too expensive."

I can understand your concern; it's a major purchase. Do you mind if I ask why you feel that way?

"I'm going to look around."

I think it is wise to look around before you make a final commitment. What is it that you hope to find?

What is the #1 reason you ask questions?

Now let's pretend you are interviewing someone for a job in which they will be reporting to you. You start off the interview by getting the interviewee comfortable, then start asking them questions. *You* are in control of the process at this point.

The interviewee answers all of your questions and thinks they are in control because they are giving good accurate answers—they are in reality selling themselves. You are impressed, as they answered all of your questions. You end the interview by telling the individual that you will get back to them. Why? Because you have other candidates to consider and want to make the right selection. Notice the similarity to the buyer's system—you the interviewer, the buyer, were in control.

Your next interview starts off the same way, with a little small talk to get the candidate comfortable, but the difference here is the candidate starts off by asking *you* questions. Rather than answering questions, they are asking questions of you and qualifying the opportunity. You in turn start answering their questions. You think you are in control, but in reality the control lies with the interviewee. The interview ends with the interviewee asking you about the next step, as opposed to you telling them.

It is now decision time. The two candidates had equal qualifications but different approaches. Which would you hire—the one who sold themselves and answered all of your questions, or the one who showed interest and asked a lot of questions?

Let's understand why the second candidate would win out. By asking questions, the candidate was showing they were interested. By listening to your responses, they made you feel important, while demonstrating their communication skills and desire to learn. The interviewer made the candidate feel important in the first interview by listening to their answers, but the candidate did not demonstrate those important questioning and listening skills or a desire to learn. They were only interested in themselves and trying to sell themselves accordingly.

Think about the way you have been approaching prospective buyers. Are you like the first candidate in the interview or the second one? Which one would you like to be?

We ask questions to stay in control of the process and to keep the prospect talking, so we can determine if there is a need that we can satisfy, while we contribute to building a long-term relationship.

The secret behind asking questions is to also have prospective buyers buy from you. Think about it. Do you prefer to be sold something or do you prefer to buy something?

Questions contribute to a self-discovery process, which is a buying process. The salesperson asks the prospect questions that lead the prospect to discover their own needs and solutions within their budget and decision-making process. They must come up with the answers themselves—you can't tell them, as they must own those answers. You just have to know what questions need to be asked in order to get the answers you are seeking.

Here are some additional tips for questioning:

Ask questions that will help you gather the types of information you need.

- Use open-ended questions when you want people to open up and talk.
- Use closed-ended questions when you need to focus the conversation, reach conclusions, etc.
- Use directing questions when you need a specific answer or need to move the conversation in a specific direction.

Use a deliberate sequence of questioning that will take you and your customer where you need to go.

- Determine what information you need.

- Use a mix of open, closed, and directing questions that will gather that information for you and keep the discussion on track.
- Constantly evaluate whether you are getting the information you need—and, if you are not, adjust your line of questioning accordingly.
- Don't assume that a customer will always "open up" with open questions, "focus in" with closed questions, etc. Be ready to rephrase questions or adjust your approach if you are not getting the answers you need, or if you are not moving the discussion in the direction it needs to go.
- Be sure that you don't give your customer the impression that he or she is being "grilled."

Listen to the answers to your questions.

- Listen 80 percent of the time. Ask questions for the other 20 percent of the time.
- Focus on what the customer is saying. Don't be thinking about your next question.
- Avoid formulating your next question while the customer is talking—particularly if that sort of activity easily distracts you from listening.
- Always question the answers for more detail. It is when you question the answer three or four levels down that you can get to the root of the problem.

Summary: Asking Questioning

- Ask questions that will help you gather the types of information you need.
- Use *open-ended* questions when you want people to open up and talk.
- Use *directing* questions when you need a specific answer or need to move the conversation in a specific direction.
- Use *fact-finding* questions to gather the information you need.
- Use *closed-ended* questions when you need to focus the conversation, reach conclusions, etc.
- Use a deliberate sequence of questioning that will take you and your prospective buyer where you need to go. Start by first identifying the solutions you provide, then the problems to which your solutions solve. Then create a list of questions you need to ask the buyer to help you uncover whether there are any problems for which you have solutions.
- Determine what information you need to qualify the buyer.
- Use a mix of open, directing, fact-finding and closed questions that will gather that information for you and keep the discussion on track.

- Constantly evaluate whether you are getting the information you need and, if you are not, adjust your line of questioning accordingly.
- Don't assume that a buyer will always "open up" with open questions, "focus in" with closed questions, etc. Be ready to rephrase questions or adjust your approach if you are not getting the answers you need, or if you are not moving the discussion in the direction it needs to go.
- Be sure that you don't give your customer the impression that he or she is being "grilled."

Questioning Techniques

- Respect-Repeat–Reverse
- Brief Answer—End with a Question
- Handling Objections
- 70/30 Rule
- The Rule of 3+
- Strip Line
- Let's Pretend
- Magic Wand
- You are on page 7 and I am on page 2
- Wishy-Washy words

Listening Skills

In the last section you learned that by asking questions you remain in control. Questions help you gain a lot more information. Questions handle objections and concerns, and questions show that you care and are interested and willing to learn more. Questions also help in self-discovery and it is the self-discovery process that gets people to buy. But there is no point in asking questions if you are not prepared to listen effectively.

You may find it difficult to listen effectively. If you are one of those people that are constantly thinking of what to ask next and not listening to the answers you are getting, you need to change. Quickly. I used to be one of those people and I changed.

First, I scripted the questions to which I needed answers and placed them in some order on a page in my notebook—a page I could refer back to when needed. That alone took some pressure off me. Then I applied the "question the answer" technique discussed in the section on asking questions. Then, rather than having to think up the next question, I would listen to what the buyer was saying and I would question *their* answer. By scripting my questions in advance and questioning the answers, I became a more effective listener. I not only learned much more by getting more information, I also earned much more respect, resulting in long-term relationships.

The other step I took to help me become a more effective listener was to monitor myself daily using the Monthly Monitor Chart. I monitored myself on two things: *"I am patient and I probe"* and *"I am an empathetic listener."* I reviewed and checked my effectiveness on these points daily. As a matter of fact, they are still on my monthly monitor because I realize how important these areas are in sales and I don't ever want to lose sight of them. You may want to consider doing the same, because being patient and probing and listening empathetically are extremely important areas to master in this sales process.

Let me explain what I mean by being an empathetic listener. People are usually sympathetic; they feel sorry about something that may have happened such as the loss of a loved one. Sympathy means you feel what your buyer feels. If you feel that your price is too high or that your terms are unreasonable, just like the client, then you have crossed the line. Sympathy (in sales) is bad. Sympathy means you are no longer capable of working out an effective solution, or more typically, of attempting to sell value.

However, to be empathetic is quite different. To demonstrate empathy is tough at first, but once mastered, it will make the biggest difference in your relationships and hence in your sales results.

Empathy means you understand. Empathy does not necessarily mean you agree with the buyer; it simply means you know what they are talking about. Empathy is good. Empathy forces you to look at the situation/objection from the buyer's perspective. It forces you to pause and to think creatively for a solution or proper response.

To be an empathetic listener you must place yourself in the other person's shoes. This may sound easy but it is not, because before you put yourself in their shoes, you must first take off *your* shoes. What I mean by that is that you must first drop or get rid of all of your preconceived ideas and assumptions. This is the most challenging part of being an empathetic listener, because it is not easy to drop all of your beliefs and go into a conversation with a totally open mind.

To be an empathetic listener you have to have a completely open mind such that you can actually experience what the other person has experienced. You must be able to see, feel and hear the experience as the other person does from their point of view. You have to be open- minded and not bound by any beliefs or past experiences. You have to be focused on listening with all of your emotions. You are living the experience as they have, not as you may have or would have.

An empathetic listener always places the buyer first, as it should be. An empathetic sales rep always sells more and makes more. Realize that, as much as you work on being an empathetic listener, there are always obstacles that have to be overcome as well—obstacles such as environmental noise, people walking by, telephones ringing and other interruptions. You have to learn to stay focused on the person you are communicating with at all times. If not, you lose.

Examples of phrasing an expression of empathy

1. I understand how your feel
2. I appreciate your concern
3. I respect your decision
4. I see why you feel that way
5. I have been there myself, so I know how you feel
6. You're right, it is a major investment
7. You're not alone – other people have said the same thing
8. That's not the first time I have heard that
9. I hear what you are saying
10. I see what you mean

There is a cost attached to ineffective communication. If you are unsure about words that are used, question them. If you are not sure that the message you communicated is clearly understood, ask that it be repeated back to you. When communicating, you can miss out on important issues and you can easily lose the buyer's trust, which in turn will destroy the relationship. Be aware of what is being said. Seek clarification and understanding at all times.

For example, in a lot of my workshops I ask the participants to identify ten words that describe what the word education means to them. When we review each participant's words, you would think there would be a common word in the group, but that is not the case. Everyone has had a different experience relating to education and will describe it from their point of view. This is true to my experience or idea; therefore, it is important to sometimes question the words someone uses to ensure total understanding of where they are coming from.

A friend of mine had such an experience. Peter owns a number of service stations and hires at least four people per location. One day an Italian fellow came along and asked Peter for a job. At the time, Peter had no opportunities and told him so. However, the Italian fellow persisted, mentioning that he had just arrived in Canada and needed work. Peter felt sorry for him and wanted to help. Peter asked him what he could do. The Italian fellow started listing a variety of jobs. As soon as Peter heard "painting," he seized the opportunity. He has a porch on the front of his house that his wife has been bugging him to get painted for over a year. Peter decided to hire the individual to paint the porch. He gave him directions to his house, told him the white paint was located behind the house in the shed, and that he should paint the porch in the front of the house with the white paint. Off he went.

At the end of the day the Italian fellow returned to the service station. Peter asked him how it was going. The Italian fellow responded that the job was done. Peter was surprised that he got it done that quickly and asked "You painted the porch in the front of the house white?" The Italian fellow responded "Yes, but there is one thing that you should be aware of. That is not a Porsche you have in front of the house; that is a Maserati." Peter almost died on the spot.

Once you experience an incident like this, your communications skills improve dramatically. Peter's have. He now has the Italian fellow working with him full time, because it was actually a joke he played on Peter. However, Peter makes sure that everything he tells him is repeated back to him for clarity and full understanding. Don't wait until your red Maserati is painted white to learn to ask for clarity in order to have a full understanding of the words people use.

As you will note from the story above, there is a cost attached to ineffective communication. If there are words used that you are not sure about, question them. If you are not sure that the message you communicated is clearly understood, ask for it to be repeated back to you. When communicating, you can miss out on important issues and you can easily lose the buyer's trust, which in turn will destroy the relationship. Be aware of what is being said. Seek clarification and understanding.

Listening is a strong relationship builder, as is questioning. Questioning shows you care and want to learn, but only if you are listening. In order for you to be effective in sales you must first understand the buyer and where they are coming from. You need to hear them out, before they will ever hear you out. By listening and getting a full understanding of their experiences and needs, you are showing the buyer respect.

Seek first to understand, if you really want to be understood.

—Stephen Covey

It is only once you fully understand the buyer that you will be in a position to relate solutions back to them in a way they can understand. Therefore, stop telling and selling. Start by asking questions and listening empathetically. Listen beyond the spoken word. You will learn a lot more, gain much more respect and build lasting relationships. It is showing that you actually care about the buyer and their needs that makes the overall difference in a relationship.

Nobody cares how much you know until they know how much you care.

—Cavett Robert

Let's take a look at some simple active listening techniques: parroting, paraphrasing, feeling feedback and demonstrating listening through our body language.

Parroting is a listening technique whereby you repeat what the client has said. It demonstrates that you heard the exact words they said.

Paraphrasing is similar but it is repeating what you heard in *your* words, not theirs.

Feeling feedback demonstrates empathy by placing yourself in their scenario and feeling the way they must have felt, and expressing that feeling back to them.

All three of these techniques can be used during your interaction with a buyer and can assist in demonstrating effective two-way communications. However, if your body language is not appropriate, these techniques are not as effective.

Body language plays a very important role in communications as it does in building rapport. Your body language speaks your mind. If you are looking at people walking by while you are having a conversation with an individual, what do you think your body is saying? Your body language, through your eye contact, is demonstrating that you are not listening to the person you are supposed to be communicating with and that you are more interested in what is going on around you than in listening to them.

Your body language always speaks your mind. Therefore, when it comes to communications that play an important role in building relationships, you need to use your body to communicate effectively. Salespeople don't normally have a problem using their body when presenting or speaking, but many do when it comes to listening.

To listen effectively, you have to show that you are interested. That means we have to focus on the person speaking. You do that by maintaining eye contact and staying focused on them and on what they are saying. You lean in and use facial expressions and nods to demonstrate concern or interest or to show continued support. Use your body to show that you are listening—it will help you listen more effectively because you are aware of what you are doing and why.

I have witnessed many characteristics of good and poor listeners and would like to share the poor ones with you so that you can avoid them. If you have any of these characteristics, get rid of them! They are not doing you any good.

A poor listener is inattentive; has wondering eyes and poor posture; always interrupts; jumps to conclusions; finishes the speaker's sentence; changes the subject; writes everything down; does not give any response; is impatient and bad-tempered; fidgets nervously with a pen, pencil or paper clip.

We talked about the wandering eyes earlier; now let's look at each of the other characteristics. Good posture reflects that you are sitting up and paying attention. If your arms are crossed and you are slouched down in your seat, you are certainly demonstrating that you are not interested. If you are constantly interrupting, jumping to conclusions or finishing sentences, as so many salespeople do, how do you think you are making the other person feel? Right. Not at all important.

You are actually making them feel you know it all and they are stupid. Is that what you want?

How do you feel when you are speaking about something and the other person changes the subject on you? Obviously they are not interested in what you are talking about and want to talk about something that is more interesting to them. Are you that type of self-centered person? If so, change, because in sales it is not about you, it is about the person in front of you, the buyer. Yes, you are the most important person in the world, but when you are with a buyer, who is the most important person? Remember, without a buyer, you cannot make a sale.

Previously I mentioned that you should bring only a note pad and a pen with you on your first sales call, but I didn't mention how you should be taking notes. If you are constantly writing everything down, you are not listening effectively. It is like being on vacation with a video camera, and being so busy taking videos of everything that you are not really enjoying what you do see. The key is to write down brief words or important points only—trigger words. When the call is over and you have left the buyer, take a few minutes to debrief and elaborate on those trigger words for future reference. Also note anything else that is worth noting away from the buyer, not in front of them. When you are with the buyer, be there 110 percent.

In the last section, you were advised to stay in control of the sales process by always asking questions and not giving any free consulting. In this section, I mentioned that a poor listener does not give any response. There is a difference between not giving free consulting and not giving any response. Not giving a response shows you are not listening. By responding using one of the listening techniques above, you are showing you at least heard them or, even better, felt for them (using the feeling feedback technique). If you do not respond to what they have been saying, you have demonstrated that you were not listening and that you don't really care what they have been saying.

If you are an impatient person, work on it. All good things come in time and you need to learn to master patience. Use your Monthly Monitor Chart and slowly you will master being patient, as I did. Don't ever lose your temper. When you do, you lose. Always. Remember you can only control the things under your control, and your temper is something that is under your control. Seek to understand as opposed to blowing up. And when listening, don't fidget with things. They only take your focus away from where it should be.

On the following pages you will find a Listening Skills Assessment Worksheet for you to complete. Please be honest with yourself and identify the areas that you need to work on, then create an action plan to improve in each of the areas that you identified as weak.

Listening Skills Assessment Worksheet

Please check mark in the appropriate circle.

	Always	Sometimes	Never
Concentration Skills			
1. When I talk with others, my mind is completely absorbed by what they are saying, and it seldom wanders.	**3**	**2**	**1**
2. When in a conversation with others, I hold my comments until they are finished talking, even though my comments may have direct relevance to what they are saying at that time.	**3**	**2**	**1**
3. I do not let distractions like ringing telephones, busy street traffic, or other conversations in a room distract my attention from what someone is saying to me.	**3**	**2**	**1**

Acknowledgment Skills

4. When talking face to face or on the phone with someone, I acknowledge what has been said with "I understand" or "I see" or other comments that let the buyer know I'm listening.	**3**	**2**	**1**

Research Skills

5. Whenever I talk with someone, I encourage the conversation and ensure that it will be a two-way flow of communication by asking open-ended questions, clarifying what I don't completely understand and giving appropriate feedback.	**3**	**2**	**1**
6. I let others know that I am listening and trying to understand what they are saying by using phrases like, "tell me more about that," or "can you give me an example?" or "then what?"	**3**	**2**	**1**

Sensing Skills

7. When I am talking with others, I read their body language as well as listen to their words, to fully interpret what they are telling me.	**3**	**2**	**1**
8. When talking with others, I try to read what is going on behind their spoken words by asking myself what they might be feeling, why they are saying what they are saying, and what the implications are.	**3**	**2**	**1**

Structuring Skills

9. Whenever I talk with others, I take either mental or written notes of the major idea, the key points, and the supporting points and/or reasons.	**3**	**2**	**1**
10. As I take my mental or written notes, I sequence — I listen for order or priority.			

Areas that I need improvement in are:

____

____

____

____

My action plan to improve in these areas is:

____

____

____

____

The 7 Tips to Effective Listening

1. Listen attentively
   - You must make the effort to concentrate on what the other person is saying, not what you're going to say next.
   - Be aware of your posture. The right posture enhances your ability to concentrate, eliminates distractions and communicates that you are listening attentively.
2. Verify your understanding
   - Pause, think about what was said, and then think about what you will say.
   - Repeat what was said using different words—without adding anything new or your interpretation.
   - Describe what you think the other person said. This is a more complex approach because it requires you to add interpretation or inference—and it requires the other person to respond to those additions.
3. Get confirmation that your verification was correct
   - The actual statement you make is only half of verifying.
   - You must ask a question requesting the confirmation.
4. Avoid appearing manipulative when seeking confirmation
   - Phrase your question in a neutral or positive way, for example, "Is that right?"
5. Seek clarification if you do not understand something
   - Don't wait.
   - Don't ignore your potential misunderstanding and risk letting it grow into an even larger misunderstanding.
6. Assume responsibility when a misunderstanding occurs
   - Don't appear to blame the other person—for any reason, no matter how ineffectively he or she seems to be communicating with you.
   - Remember that, as a salesperson, you want to build rapport. Making people feel foolish or at fault is not only rude but counterproductive.
7. Take advantage of nonverbal clues
   - Maintain eye contact and an open posture; face the other person squarely.

- Be sensitive to the kind of nonverbal clues that you receive from the other person as you apply your active listening skills.
- Verify the nonverbal "messages" that you receive.

LISTEN

When I ask you to listen to me
 and you start giving me advice
 you have not done what I have asked.
When I ask you to listen to me
 and you begin to tell me why I shouldn't feel that way,
 you are trampling on my feelings.
When I ask you to listen to me
 and you feel you have to do something to solve my problems
 you have failed me, strange as that may seem.
Listen! All I asked, was that you listen
 not talk or do – just hear me.
Advice is cheap: 10 cents will get both Dear Abby and
 Billy Graham in the same newspaper.
And I can do for myself; I'm not helpless.
 Maybe discouraged and faltering, but not helpless.
When you do something for me that I can and need to do
 for myself, you contribute to my fear and weakness.
But, when you accept as a simple fact that I do feel what I feel,
 no matter how irrational, then I can quit trying to convince
 you and get about the business of understanding what's
 behind this irrational feeling. And when that's clear, the answers
 are obvious and I don't need advice
Irrational feelings don't make sense when we understand what's behind them.
Perhaps that's why prayer works sometimes, for some people,
 because God is mute, and he doesn't give advice or try to fix things.
"They" just listen and let you work it out for yourself.
So, please listen and just hear me. And, if you want to talk,
 Wait a minute for your turn; and I'll listen to you.

—Anonymous

Summary of Listening Skills

- Be aware of the barriers to effective listening and how to overcome them.
- "Seek first to understand, if you really want to be understood." Stephen Covey
- "Nobody cares how much you know until they know how much you care." Cavett Robert
- Parroting— repeat what the client has said.
- Paraphrasing—similar to parroting but it is repeating what you heard in *your* words, not theirs.
- Feeling feedback—feeling the way they must have felt, and expressing that feeling back to them.
- Be aware of your body language, maintain eye contact, use encouraging facial expressions and body movements to demonstrate active listening. Know and demonstrate the characteristics of effective listeners.

Buyer Empowerment

Buyer empowerment means giving buyers the power, or authority, to buy. This is the opposite of traditional sales techniques where salespeople believed they were empowered to "sell" everyone. However, salespeople need to realize that not everyone is qualified.

Buyer empowerment comes from asking, not telling. Nobody likes to be told what to do. However, everyone loves to be asked. Everyone likes to be empowered. It is a sign of trust.

The simple act of engaging buyers, with the asking of questions and listening to the answers, empowers the buyer. Being empowered also makes the buyer feel important, understood, comfortable and welcomed—the universal needs of buyers.

Your job is to ask the right questions to empower the buyer to qualify and buy your product or service solutions. When buyers are empowered through your questioning and listening techniques they discover their own needs, budgets, decision, timing and appropriate solutions to solve those needs. Overall, you are empowering the buyer to qualify, or not, to buy your solutions.

Each salesperson has different opportunities to qualify during any day, and these opportunities come in a variety of forms, at different times of the day. If you are not ready to qualify these opportunities when they come along, you lose.

Simply taking the time to properly qualify a prospective buyer, by asking intelligent questions is a value-added service that most salespeople don't offer. Too many salespeople just want to sell and forget about properly qualifying the buyer, let alone empowering the buyer to qualify. Selling without qualifying is like a doctor who gives you a prescription without first diagnosing the problem.

When you have an opportunity to qualify a prospective buyer, what is it that you really want? The answer you will get from most salespeople is "an order" or "a yes." But that is not the only answer you should be looking for when you empower the buyer to qualify.

As a salesperson, your job is to qualify prospective buyers. It is your responsibility to determine whether the buyer is qualified to do business with you, or not. In most cases, the opposite takes place. It is the buyer who qualifies the salesperson and their products or services. It is the salesperson who usually gets rejected, isn't it?

When using the "Buyer Focused" Velocity Selling System you are in control of the selling process and you will determine if the prospect is qualified or not, and it is up to you to reject the buyer, while maintaining the relationship, not the other way around.

There are **five positive outcomes** to a sales call, or buyer encounter as I prefer to call it. The first positive outcome to a buyer encounter is an obvious one—a **yes,** the buyer qualifies and buys your solutions.

However, if the buyer is not qualified, a **no**, is also a positive outcome. How much time have you wasted in the past on people who are not qualified to buy? You know that sales is a numbers game and you have to get through so many no's to get to a yes, so why not get through the no's quickly. Why would you want to waste your time on someone who is not qualified to buy from you anyway? Is a "no" not also a positive outcome?

If you don't get a yes, or a no, there is a third option, and it is not a maybe. Maybe is a wishy-washy word that has no clarity or meaning. What you need to do is secure what I call a **clear future**. A clear future is exactly what it says— what is going to happen next and when. A clear future is a clearly defined plan of action, committed to by the prospective buyer, of the next steps in the process—steps that you agree are also important to proceed toward a yes or a no.

If you don't get a yes, a no, or a clear future, you then have to find a **lesson learned,** because you failed to secure one of the above three outcomes. A lesson learned means going back over the system and determining where you went wrong and what you can do better the next time to prevent the same thing from happening again.

The fifth and final positive outcome of an opportunity is to always ask for a **referral or an introduction**. Remember, one of your rights is to ask. If you don't ask, you don't get. It is your responsibility as a salesperson to ask. Make it a habit to always ask for a referral or an introduction from every qualifying opportunity, no matter what the outcome is.

Throughout the entire Velocity Selling System the buyer is being engaged and empowered to make decisions and take ownership. As the buyer is engaged, through the asking of questions by the salesperson, the buyer *feels* they are in control, or empowered to answer the questions or make decisions. When the answer is the buyer's, they own it. Ownership is buyer empowerment. While control remains with the person asking the questions, the person answering the questions feels they are in control.

That is why it is so important not to be telling, but asking. If the answer comes from the salesperson, they own it, not the buyer. The buyer will then be in control, while the salesperson thinks they are in control. When the buyer is not empowered to take ownership, they don't buy. They use excuses like "I'll get back to you," or "Let me think about it," and end up wasting your time.

Each of the first two steps of the "Buyer Focused" Velocity Selling System is engaging and empowering the buyer. This requires the salesperson to be asking questions 30 percent of the time and listening attentively the other 70 percent of the time. There is no room for you, the salesperson, to be talking.

Only in the third step, Prescribing Solutions, can you actually be talking and sharing your knowledge in relationship to the needs identified, providing you have a qualified buyer who made a commitment to you prior to the presentation—a yes or no answer after your presentation. And even then, the buyer is empowered to say yes or no, as you will be in the summary step, providing you set it up properly in the setting-the-parameters step.

Enough teasing, let's get on to Part 2 and dive into the "Buyer Focused" Velocity Selling System.

Summary—Buyer Empowerment

- The simple act of engaging buyers, with the asking of questions and listening to the answers, is empowering the buyer. Being empowered also makes the buyer feel important, understood, comfortable and welcomed—the universal needs of buyers.
- Positive outcomes of a buyer encounter:
  1. Yes. The buyer is qualified and buys.
  2. No. The buyer is not qualified and rejected but a relationship is maintained.
  3. A clear future—you know exactly what is going to happen next.

4. Lesson learned—you failed to achieve one of the about three.
5. Ask for a referral. If you don't ask, you don't get.

Review and Daily Disciplines for Competencies: the "Buyer Focused" Velocity Selling System, Part 1

In "Competencies, Part 1," you learned the four steps on how buyers buy and how they are in control of the sales process most of the time, particularly when the salespeople themselves are not following a sales process.

You also learned the four universal needs of buyers and created lists on what you can do to satisfy these needs.

Then you learned the three most important competencies you need to master first before using the Velocity Selling System.

You learned how to be buyer focused, how to engage buyers through two important communication skills—asking questions and listening, which in turn allow you to realize the third competency, buyer empowerment.

Once again, you learned a lot. All that is left to do is for you to reflect on all of the learning you received and the examples provided. It is now time to write out the daily disciplines you want to instil in your life and then do what you have to do. Remember that any behavior that gets recognized or rewarded gets repeated, so include the behaviors as well.

Daily Disciplines:

What did you learn?

____

____

____

____

1. What daily disciplines do you want to apply for yourself?

____

____

____

____

What will your reward be for doing what you say you will do?

____

____

2. What daily disciplines do you want to implement toward your Organization?

What will your reward be for doing what you say you will do?

3. What daily disciplines do you want to apply toward buyers?

What will be your reward for doing what you say you will do?

Reminder: review these disciplines daily for the next twenty-one consecutive days, or use the Monthly Monitor Chart for twenty-five out of thirty-one days and you will make these disciplines effective habits.

COMPETENCIES—THE "BUYER FOCUSED" VELOCITY SELLING SYSTEM, PART 2

1. Building Relationships
    1. Building Rapport
    2. Understanding Dominant Senses

2. Qualifying Buyer Opportunities
    1. Setting Parameters (ground rules)
    2. Uncovering Buying Motivators
    3. Uncovering Financial Ability
    4. Uncovering Decision Making
    5. Summarizing

3. Prescribing Solutions
    1. Prescribed Presentations
    2. Let the Buyer Buy
    3. Eliminating Potential Back Outs

4. Maintaining Buyer Relationships
    1. Exceed Expectations While Providing Added Value

Competencies—the "Buyer Focused" Velocity Selling System, Part 2

Think about a present relationship you have with a client, a partner, a spouse or a friend. How did you get it started? Try to remember your first encounter and what happened that started that relationship. Next, think about what you did to keep that relationship going?

Did your success have anything to do with asking questions, listening and discovering commonalities while showing you cared? You bet it did.

In this series of chapters we are going to discover how to build and maintain long-term relationships. Relationships between people like you and me. You must first understand that people buy from people, particularly people they trust and like—people who remind them of themselves. Therefore, it is important for you to be aware of and to understand the person with whom you are building a relationship.

As mentioned earlier, the objective should not be to make a sale, but to establish a relationship and to qualify the buyer to determine if there is an opportunity to do business, or not. Making a sale is secondary. If the buyer is not qualified, you cannot help him. However, because you have established a relationship, they may be in a position to refer you to others who are qualified. They become your secondary sales force.

> *Sales is a people business and it is all about relationships. The more relationships you have, the bigger your network will be. The bigger your network, the bigger your Net Worth.*
>
> —**Bob Urichuck**

In the next section you will learn how to build rapport quickly so that you can gain the trust that is needed to ask questions and get answers. You will need to use two basic communications skills: the skill of asking questions and the skill of listening to the responses, as learned in previous chapters. What is the point of asking questions if you are too busy thinking up other questions to ask, and not listening? You will also learn how to identify a person's dominant sense so that you can better relate to them in the way they see, feel or hear—the emotional triggers.

At one time we were taught to follow the golden rule "Do unto others as you would have them do unto you." That was a great rule to follow. It is right to say that, to yourself, you are the most important person in the world and under the golden rule, how you treat yourself is how you should also treat others.

However, over the years the golden rule has been replaced with the platinum rule: "Do unto others as they would like to have done unto themselves." The platinum rule takes on a different approach. What it is saying is that when you are with another person, treat them the way **they** would like to be treated, not the way you would want to be treated. Therefore, we have had to change our approach.

When we meet with a buyer as a salesperson, who is the most important person in the world? I hope you said the opposite of the golden rule and said the buyer. If so, great, because without a buyer, you have absolutely no chance of selling them anything. Do you agree? I hope so.

So, if the buyer is the most important person in the world when selling and we are to follow the platinum rule, we had better treat them the way they want to be treated. That means we have to be on our toes and look for all kinds of clues, clues that I will share with you shortly. But first let's look at the way we approach buyers, considering the universal needs of buyers.

First of all, would you agree that it is a privilege to be invited to a buyer's office?

Good, I certainly agree with you that it is a great privilege. But take note of the words that I used in my question. Do you use the word "invite" or do you make appointments with buyers? Simply changing a few words in our language can change the scenario.

Let's go back to the initial telephone call, if that is how you get invited to a buyer's place of business. First of all let's understand that a telephone call is an intrusion and we must approach it as such. When you make the call, do you quickly introduce yourself, state your unique benefit statement and ask if this is a good time to talk before proceeding? If the answer is yes, do you also ask permission to ask questions? If you do, you are on the right track. If not, start asking if it is a good time to talk and seek permission to ask questions. If it is not a good time, ask what a good time would be to call back, and call back then.

By asking a few simple pre-planned questions, within the first three minutes you should be able to identify if the buyer is qualified to meet or not. If they are qualified, rather than saying, "I would like to meet with you and show you how we can satisfy your need, or provide a solution to your problem." try saying something like, "Do you ever invite people like myself to your office to discuss these problems, and possible solutions, in greater detail?" You will get a yes most of the time, and by asking to be invited you are setting a different tone for the meeting. Then, of course, when you arrive at the meeting, you thank them for inviting you.

Now you are at the meeting. What did you bring with you? Did you bring a bag full of information, a brochure, some samples, etc.? I hope not, because if you did, you will automatically lose control. The buyer will want to see what you have in the bag and you will want to show them everything in it.

The secret of a first call is to go in with nothing more than a note pad and a pen or pencil. This initial phase is to build trust and to make the prospect feel important and comfortable with you.

Once rapport has been established and the buyer is comfortable and open with you, set the parameters of the meeting—Qualifying Buyer Opportunities, step 2, making the buyer more comfortable, while eliminating surprises.

Then you need to question, or engage and empower the buyer to determine if there are any buying motivators for your products or services. You need to know what questions you must ask them here to fully uncover three or four problems or buying motivators. If they have no reason to buy, they are not going to buy. No pain, no gain; therefore they are not qualified, at present, to buy.

However, if there are reasons to buy, you need to find out if they have any money to pay for the products or services you may have that could help them. In other words, determine their financial ability. You also need to know when they will be making that decision to buy and who will be making that decision. These are all qualifiers, answers that you need before you can give any information away.

Once you have all of this information you can then summarize, also in step 2 of Qualifying Buyer Opportunities, and determine if there is an opportunity to do business or not. If you can solve their buying motivators or problems, within their budget and time frame, you then have a qualified opportunity and can proceed to step 3: Prescribing Solutions. If you can't, there is no sense in proceeding. The prospect is simply not qualified to receive a presentation. You abort, maintain the relationship and seek out referrals and introductions.

Step 4, the final step, is maintaining the buyer relationship after the purchase and developing what I call a secondary sales force.

Building A Long-Term Relationship

The Relationship Selling Model

AN INVESTMENT 1. Time 2. Energy 3. Ability 4. Money 5. Status (reputation)

+

GENUINE SINCERE ASSISTANCE

+

TRUST

=

RELATIONSHIP A commitment from both parties

1. BUILDING RELATIONSHIPS

Building Rapport

rap·port (from the Old French "to bring back")
1: relationship 2: agreement 3: harmony
—Webster's Dictionary

In order to build a relationship, you must consider a number of factors. The first must be to establish trust. Trust can be established in a number of ways, but the quickest way is through building rapport. Once rapport is established and the prospect trusts you, you can proceed to ask questions and get information. Without trust, the prospect will not answer any questions. This is the most important first step in the Velocity Selling System that you are about to learn.

In contemporary use, "building rapport" refers to achieving a sense of relationship, agreement and harmony. However, the word "rapport" actually derives from Old French and means "to bring back." In sales, the concept of "bringing back" is key to what is meant by "building rapport."

Building rapport is an ongoing process that is only beginning early in the sales effort. Therefore, you will have both *short-range* and *longer-range* objectives for building rapport.

Objectives

These are some typical *short-range* objectives for building rapport:

- Make the buyer comfortable in the sales situation.
- Begin to find out why the buyer is there—gain a sense of the buyer's need and how you can learn more about that need.
- Ensure that you will be able to continue the sales effort beyond its opening moments.

Objectives such as these must be met if you expect the buyer to be around long enough for you to earn the right to proceed.

Here are some typical *longer-range* objectives for building rapport:

- Gain attention so that you are able to begin a dialogue with the buyer.
- Begin building a foundation of rapport between yourself and the buyer—the sense of "harmony, affinity, and agreement" that is key to your success.
- Earn the right to proceed—ensuring that the prospect will stay with you and return if necessary, thus positioning yourself to learn about the prospect's need and complete the sale.

The Rapport Pie was developed through the study of neurolinguistic programming (NLP) by Drs. Bandler and Grinder. "Neuro" (from the Greek "neuron" – nerve) denotes your nervous system, which makes you feel well when your body is in harmony or "out of sync" when you feel ill. "Linguistic" (from the Latin "lingua") denotes the way you communicate. Programming is the system or organizational pattern needed to achieve a desired result.

NLP is literally the science of how to most effectively communicate with your brain and nervous system to produce various behavioral results. The most important skill for a salesperson is the ability to communicate. Through the use of NLP strategies you will learn how to be a better communicator, view a situation from the other person's point of view and build rapport in a short period of time.

The Rapport Pie

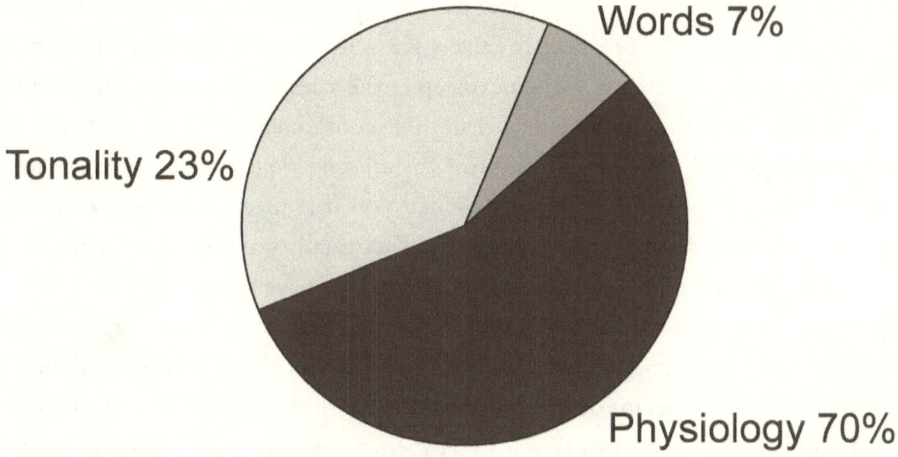

You will note that the most important piece of the rapport pie (70 percent) is physiology— your physical body. What this means is that your physical body has more to do with building rapport than the tone of your voice or the words that you use. Physiology can be used, and is very important, in face-to-face situations.

At 23 percent, tonality ranks second in building rapport. Tonality is the tone of our voice, high to low. It is also the rate of our speech, slow to fast. Tonality is most important when working on the phone.

Words represent the smallest portion of the rapport pie, at seven percent. Yet how much emphasis have you placed on words alone in the past? The words you used probably did you more harm than good.

So, where should we be focusing our efforts to quickly build rapport? Not on words, but on physiology. And the way to do that is through a technique that is referred to as matching and mirroring. Matching and mirroring is simply taking notice of the prospect's body language, tonality and words, then mirroring, matching or reflecting them back to the buyer.

Earlier I mentioned that people buy from people, particularly people they trust and like—people who remind them of themselves. When you match and mirror, the buyer sees himself or herself in you, making them more comfortable with you. However, you must also understand that matching and mirroring does differ from mimicking. Mimicking is doing as they do *when* they do it. That is not what we are talking about. You take notice of the way the person opposite you sits, stands, walks, talks and the words they use. You simply match and mirror them over time, not at the exact same time. Many salespeople do this naturally and don't even know they are doing it. They make prospective buyers very comfortable first by matching and mirroring and then move on to the next step of the sales cycle. But, we are not there yet. Let's take some time to understand all three components of the rapport pie.

Physiology is the biggest contributor to building rapport and there are many ways to match and mirror physiology. When you first meet someone, what is the first thing that you do with them, physically? You usually walk up to them and shake their hand. When we shake hands with someone, we have always been told to have a firm grip. Now pretend for a moment that the person you are meeting has a very soft handshake and you give them a firm grip. Do you think you make them feel comfortable and important or overpowered and intimidated? The answer: the latter. What is important in this first step is to let them squeeze your hand first and within a second, match that same squeeze back.

I use this technique all the time, especially when I speak before large audiences. I will greet people at the door as they come in. They don't even know who I am most of the time and I am just standing there greeting them and shaking their hands. The funny thing is I am matching all of their handshakes and starting to build rapport with them. When I get introduced and appear on stage, they are saying to themselves, "Hey, I know him, he was the guy at the door; he is just like me." Why? Because I made them feel comfortable with me by matching their handshake.

There are many other physical acts that can be mirrored and matched. You can walk at the same pace as the other person, stand like they do, sit, lean, point or match their hand and facial gestures. The most important part is that they see themselves in you, without you mimicking them. So be aware of the other person's physiology, and over time, mirror and match.

Tonality can be matched by speaking at the same rate and the same pitch. This technique is similar to the handshake. How do you think a soft slow-speaking person will feel with someone who is a loud fast talker? Do you think the buyer is feeling comfortable?

When doing telephone work, tonality is your greatest asset because it is the person at the other end that answers the phone and speaks first. You have to clue in and match their tone and pace. Mind you, although they can't see your physiology, you should still be standing tall and speaking up. Too many salespeople lean on their arm on the desk, holding the phone and speaking down. They sound depressed. Try standing up and looking at yourself in a mirror on the ceiling and you will notice how much better your voice sounds. You will find that it is clearer, more confident and enthusiastic.

Although words play a small part in building rapport, they are still important to match and mirror. All you have to do is listen to the words the buyer is using and use them yourself. Listen for and use their buzz words and their terminology. For example, if they refer to a hotel as a resort, use the word resort. If they say "correct" or "right" a lot, use the word "correct" or "right" with them when you are speaking.

Now, how are you going to remember the prospects physiology, tonality and words? What do you have with you on your first call? Right, only a notebook and a pen or pencil. Use them, in this case, after the meeting to help remember these things.

Your objective at this stage is to ask open-ended questions, to get the buyer to open up, to talk. So, what do people like to talk about the most? Themselves.

Get the buyer talking about themselves and keep them talking, while you mirror and match their physiology, tonality and words. Listen to them, question their answers, show interest and concern and keep them talking. The more they talk, the more you listen, the more you learn, the more they will like you, trust you and buy from you. You will know when you have rapport when the buyer is communicating openly with you, and can't stop talking.

Remember, it is all about the buyer—not you, your organization, products or services, features or benefits.

Understanding Dominant Senses

Now let's move on to another component of understanding people: determining their dominant sense. As you know, we have five dominant senses: sight, sound, touch, smell and taste. Research has proven that the three dominant senses of the five are sight (visual), sound (auditory) and touch (kinesthetic) and that each of us possesses one of these senses as a dominant sense and one as a secondary sense.

When we take the time to understand and determine the dominant sense of the other person we are in contact with, we can change our language and presentation style to improve communications. By using visual words and visuals we can better relate with visual people. The same applies to those whose dominant sense is auditory and to those who are kinesthetic.

First let's take a look at people who are dominantly visual.

Visual people see the world. Everything is sight-based. Even when they speak they see the picture in the mind's eye and speak to the picture. Because of this, visual people usually speak fast; they often don't finish their sentences because they are on to the next picture in their mind. Visual people also have a good visual memory and are good with directions.

It is very important for us to listen to the type of words the other person is using. Visual people will use visual phrases, like "picture this," "show me how it works" or "see what I mean."

To appeal to and to communicate effectively with a visual person, you must show them your product or service using visual words and, of course, visuals— pictures, PowerPoint and/or flip chart presentations. Remember, they have a need to see the way things are.

Visual Cues

Predicates
see show bright picture clear look envision view
perceive illustrate highlight focus reflect watch
preview survey perspective

Eye Movements
Up and **right**— *thinking about the future*
Up and **left**— *thinking about the past*
Unfocused/staring— *synthesizing thoughts—converting words into images*

Visual Characteristics
Maintains good eye contact
Voice high pitched and fast
Good with directions
Good visual memory

Unlike visual people who *see* the world, auditory people *hear* the world. To an auditory person the words used are the most important. Auditory people use phrases like "hear this," "tell me how it works," "do you hear what I am saying?" Auditory people will structure the sentence in their mind, repeat it to themselves a few times and then speak it slowly and accurately. Why? Simply because words are so important to them, as sounds are.

To appeal to and to communicate effectively with an auditory person, you must tell them about your product or service using auditory words and, of course, documentation—specifications, warranties, procedures, etc. Remember, they have a need to hear or read the way things are, not see the way things are.

Auditory Cues

Predicates
say tell tone static ring sound speak
express mention accent resonate remark
ask inquire hear talk

Eye Movements
Side right—*thinking about the future*
Side left—*thinking about the past*
Down left—*synthesizing thoughts—converting words to sound*

Auditory Characteristics
Lower-pitched voice, rhythmic & smooth
Try to sound good
Like concerts and music; self-talk

Unlike visual and auditory people who see and hear the world, kinesthetic people *feel* the world. To a kinesthetic person touch and feelings are the most important. Kinesthetic people use phrases like "it feels good," "I sense how it works," "do you know what I am saying?" Kinesthetic people will feel hot or cold about you. Why? Simply because feelings, or gut instinct, are so important to them, as is touch.

To appeal to and to communicate effectively with a kinesthetic person, you must appeal more to their emotions about your product or service using kinesthetic words and, of course, samples they can touch and feel. Remember, they have a need to touch and feel the way things are, not see or hear the way things are.

Kinesthetic Cues

Predicates
feel grab touch handle rub grasp affect
impress hit suffer tackle pressure know

Eye Movement
Down right – *synthesizing thoughts—converting words to feelings*

Kinesthetic Characteristics
Feel hot or cold about you
Frequent pauses in conversation
Like to touch people

You now need to take some time to decide what *your* dominant sense is and your secondary sense. Once you know your dominant and secondary sense you will note that it is a lot easier to communicate with a person who also has the same dominant senses, and more challenging with those whose dominant sense you do not have.

Allow me to share my senses with you, so you understand where I am coming from and what challenges I face. You may have similar challenges that you need to be aware of.

I am a visual–kinesthetic type of person. It is easy for me to understand and quickly bond with other visual and kinesthetic types of people. However, my challenge is more with auditory people. As a visual, I speak quickly and as a kinesthetic, I speak from the heart and reveal my feelings. When communicating with an auditory person, I have to learn to slow down and fully enunciate my words. Also, because words are important to auditory people I have to make sure I don't make any spelling mistakes and speak more slowly than I do with visual people. The other challenge is for me not to complete their sentences, as I see too many visual (sales) people doing this. Not only is it rude, it is creating communication barriers, destroying potential relationships and killing a potential sale.

In order to communicate effectively and to build relationships, you have to learn to communicate in all three senses, in a manner that is consistent with the other person's dominant sense. It is not always easy, but if you take the time to listen, you will find that it does become easier.

Understanding the other person's dominant sense will come in very handy toward the end of the sales process when you are making your presentation in step 3, Prescribing Solutions. However, it is better to mention it here so that you can start listening for clues now! There are excellent materials available on Neuro-Linguistic Programming NLP that go into much greater detail on visual, auditory and kinesthetic characteristics, related eye movements, and so on.

Complete the Preference Survey on the next two pages to identify your dominant and secondary senses.

Visual / Auditory / Kinesthetic—Preference Survey

In the list below, check (✓) the **A, B,** *or* **C** response that appeals most to you.

There are no correct or incorrect answers. You are simply selecting *your* personal choice. This survey helps ascertain whether your predominant mode is ***auditory***, ***visual***, or ***kinesthetic***. The checked letters will later be totaled to determine your perceptual preference.

1. A ____ I love to listen to music.
B ____ I enjoy art galleries and window shopping.
C ____ I feel compelled to dance to a good music.

2. A ____ I would rather take an oral test than a written test.
B ____ I was good at spelling at school.
C ____ I tend to answer test questions using my "gut".

3. A ____ I have been told I have a great speaking voice.
B ____ My confidence increases when I look good.
C ____ I enjoy being touched.

4. A ____ I can resolve problems more quickly when I talk out loud.
B ____ I prefer to be shown an illustration than to have something explained to me.
C ____ I find myself holding or touching things as they are being explained to me.

5. A ____ I can usually determine sincerity by the sound of a person's voice.
B ____ I find myself evaluating others based on appearance.
C ____ The way others shake my hand means a lot to me.

6. A ____ I would rather listen to cassettes than to read books.
B ____ I like to watch television and go to the movies.
C ____ I like hiking and outdoor activities.

7. A ____ I can hear even the slightest noise that my car makes.
B ____ It's important that my car is kept clean, inside out.
C ____ I like a car that feels good when I drive it.

8. A ____ Others tell me that I am easy to talk to.
B ____ I enjoy "people watching."
C ____ I tend to touch people when talking.

9. A ____ I can easily tell from the voice on the phone, who is on the other end of the line.
B ____ I often remember what someone looked like, but not the person's name.
C ____ I can't remember what people look like.

10. A ____ I often find myself humming or singing to the radio.
B ____ I enjoy photography.
C ____ I like to make things with my hands.

11. A ____ I would rather have an idea explained to me than to read it.
B ____ I enjoy speakers more if they use visual aids.
C ____ I like to participate in activities rather than watch.

12. A ____ I am a good listener.
B ____ I find myself evaluating others based on appearance.
C ____ I feel positive or negative toward others, sometimes without knowing why.

13. A ____ I can resolve problems more quickly when I talk out loud.
B ____ I am good at finding my way using a map.
C ____ I exercise because of the way I feel afterward.

14. A ____ I like a house with rooms that allow for quiet areas.
B ____ It's important that my house is clean and tidy.
C ____ I like a house that feels comfortable.

15. A ____ I like to try to imitate the way people talk.
B ____ I make a list of things I need to do each day.
C ____ I've been told that I'm well-coordinated.

Total the number of ***A***, ***B*** and ***C*** responses and record your score below.

Total # of ***A*** responses: ____________
Total # of ***B*** responses: ____________
Total # of ***C*** responses: ____________

The letter assigned to the individual modes are as follows:
A = auditory mode ***B = visual mode*** ***C = kinesthetic mode***

A high score of ***A*** responses indicates an ***auditory*** preference. Scoring more ***B*** responses indicates a ***visual*** preference and a high score of ***C*** responses indicates that you have a ***kinesthetic*** preference.

My perceptual preference, (*based on this questionnaire*) **is** ________________.

Besides senses, there are also other areas you should be observing. There are many hints you can get from physical surroundings, mannerisms, physical appearances and characteristic traits. They are all worth taking note of, in your notebook, after you leave the buyer. But there is a word of caution, don't make any assumptions. A messy desk does not always mean that the person is disorganized. However, it *would* tell me not just to leave a brochure but to review it with him or her first.

Remember your objective in this first step of the "Buyer Focused" Velocity Selling System is to build rapport. To do that is to ask open-ended questions—to get the buyer to open up, to talk. So, what do people like to talk about the most?

Themselves.

Get the buyer talking about themselves and keep them talking, while you mirror and match their physiology, tonality and words. Listen to them, question their answers, show interest and concern, determine their dominant senses as best you can, but keep them talking. The more they talk, the more you listen, the more you learn, the more they will like you, trust you and buy from you. You will know when you have rapport when the buyer is communicating openly with you, and can't stop talking.

Remember, it is all about the buyer—not you, your organization, products or services, features or benefits.

Rapport-Building Questions

Here are some sample questions you can ask to build rapport:

Tell me about your…
What type of work do you do?
How long have you been doing that?
What do you enjoy most about it?
What kind of movies do you enjoy?
What music do you prefer?
Who is your favorite artist / group?
What kind of car do you drive?
How do you like it?
How old are your children?
What are their names?
Where are you going on your vacation?
What sports interest you?

Summary

- Ask if it is a good time to talk; if not, reschedule the call.
- Ask permission to ask questions and/or take notes.

- When setting appointments, ask to be *invited.*
- Adopt the relationship-selling model.
- Mirror and match the components of the Rapport Pie—physiology 70 percent, tonality 23 percent, words 7 percent—to build rapport.
- Match and mirror. Don't mimic people with whom you want to build rapport.
- Know your dominant sense and identify the other person's dominant senses: visual, auditory, kinesthetic
- Observe and take note of the physical surroundings/appearance, mannerism, traits.
- Ask rapport-building questions. Get the buyer talking and keep them talking. The more they talk, the more you listen, the more you learn and the more they will like you and trust you.

2. QUALIFYING BUYER OPPORTUNITIES

Setting Parameters

Once rapport has been established you can move on to Qualifying Buyer Opportunities, step 2 of the Velocity Selling System. Remember this is a step-by-step system and each step must be completed before moving on to the next step. So, how do you know when you have established rapport and can move on to step 2?

Quite simply, when you know the buyer is comfortable with you. They have opened up and are talking a lot about themselves. When you witness this happening, you can then move on to step 2. First, let's provide you with some background on the first step of qualifying buyer opportunities—setting parameters.

To qualify buyer opportunities you must first set the parameters of your meeting to eliminate surprises and create an environment of trust, honesty and openness. This is where you create additional trust and make the buyer feel more comfortable with you. Too many salespeople don't do this and leave the buyer feeling uncomfortable and nervous throughout the whole meeting.

Setting the parameters of a meeting is not new. It exists in all professions, including sports. It is simply setting the ground rules of how the parties are going to interact during the course of the meeting or play. The nice thing about setting the parameters is that it eliminates surprises and makes everyone feel much more comfortable.

Naturally, to do this you may have to change your traditional ways and realize something important right up front. Earlier we talked about the most important person in the world. I am sure you agreed that it was you. However, when we are with a prospective buyer, whom do you believe the most important person should be?

Hopefully you responded with the prospective buyer being the most important person. Remember one thing, that without a buyer, you have no opportunity for doing business. Therefore, when you are with a buyer, make sure they are treated as the most important person in the world, and you can do this by engaging and empowering them in setting the parameters.

Your first objective is simply to meet with a prospective buyer to determine whether there is an opportunity to do business or not. Whatever the outcome, your objective would still be to establish a relationship. Therefore you still follow the system and build rapport. Once you feel you have established rapport and the customer is feeling comfortable with you, you are ready to get down to business and set the parameters.

But what parameters should be set, you ask? Good question; let's start by putting ourselves in the shoes of prospective buyers, and ask "What would make anyone feel comfortable in a meeting between a buyer and a salesperson"

There are a few things that make most people more comfortable, like the amount of time allocated to the meeting, the objective or outcomes, the agenda and/or possible next steps, permission to ask questions and take notes, and the list can go on.

The real secret in setting these parameters is to not tell the prospective buyer what the parameters are but to engage and empower the buyer by asking them what they should be. When they are the buyer's answers, he/she owns them and will respect them. If you tell them, they are your parameters, not theirs. It is most important that they feel they are taking ownership of the meeting at the outset. It has to be their ideas. This is how they will feel they are in control. You will still have an opportunity to add yours, but only after they have stated theirs.

You can start to set the parameters after you know you have established rapport and the buyer is open with you.

Review the sample questions I am providing to you below. Take each of them, and put them into your words, and use them as part of your daily buyer encounters in setting parameters.

Here is an example that you can use to get the conversation going, simply by asking a question:

Salesperson: "John, how much time have you set aside for our meeting today?"

Buyer: "Thirty minutes."

The first question on time empowers the buyer to confirm the amount of time available for the meeting—it could be longer than originally planned if the first step, building rapport, went well and if additional time is available. Hopefully the answer will be what was previously agreed to or more time. If so, *great!* If less time is provided, question why and reschedule for the amount of time you need if there is not enough time, or try to do the little bit that you can in the amount of time provided to qualify the prospect. Don't try to do something you know requires a larger amount of time. Reschedule. If you try to do it in less time, you will probably lose.

Now that you have confirmed the amount of time available to you, you can simply ask the prospect what their objectives, or outcomes, of the meeting are, and even set an agenda.

Remember that objectives and outcomes are the end results of a meeting and you are striving to find out *their* end result, not yours. Yes, traditional sales has always told you to go into a sales call with an objective, and there is nothing wrong with that. The difference here is whose objectives are more important, yours or the buyer's? If you are buyer focused, as recommended, it would be the buyer's. You can always add your objective, after the buyer has stated theirs.

For example:

Salesperson: "What is it that you would like to accomplish in the next thirty minutes, John?"

Buyer: "To learn about some of the solutions you may have that can help me solve..."

Salesperson: "Thanks, John, and I would also like to learn more about you and your organization to see if there is an opportunity to do business together, or not. Is it okay if we ask each other questions?"

Buyer: "Yes."

Salesperson: "Do you mind if I take some notes as we go?"

Buyer: "Go right ahead."

Note the way the buyer's objective is first, followed by yours, along with permission to ask questions and take notes. Make this a courtesy habit with everyone you meet. With permission to ask questions, you get answers. Only once have I been told not to take notes due to privacy matters. Both show that you are interested in the buyer while making them feel important.

You can also ask; *Did you want to set an agenda?* If so, let them lead the way. Add in your agenda items as you go. You may also want to ask *What would be the next step if we don't get to all the items listed on the agenda?* Always strive to get a clear future and a commitment from the prospect every step along the way.

A word of caution—however you ask the questions or lead the prospective buyer, be yourself. Ask questions your way and have some fun. Don't take qualifying so seriously. Buyers are stressed enough as it is. Try to inject some humor along the way. The more they laugh the more the barriers come down.

Now you have just confirmed or learned some obvious things in setting parameters for a meeting. Now, let's take it a step closer to the real world of sales. One of the biggest fears buyers have of salespeople is that they are going to sell them something, something they probably don't want. How do we get around this fear, so that they could let their barriers down, have some fun and be more relaxed and receptive?

Traditional sales training has always told us to go for a "yes." In sales you know that you cannot satisfy everyone's needs and that your responsibility is to also reject clients, and that they can also reject you.

As a matter of fact, you are probably getting more no's than yes's as it is. We have already agreed that a no is a positive outcome of a qualifying opportunity. We also know that it takes many no's to get a yes. Therefore, let's take control, change our attitude and go for the opposite. Let's go for a "no" instead of a "yes." By doing so, what do you think will happen with the prospective buyer? Do you think their barriers may come down, they may have some fun and that they may be more relaxed and receptive?

Simply say something like:

Salesperson: "Before I get started, John, I don't know if I can help you or not, as I cannot solve all of the world's problems. If I feel I cannot help you, is it ok if I tell you No, I can't? However, if I can, I will tell you Yes, I can.

"Can we be honest with each other and work on a no or yes basis, as I don't want to waste your time?

How does this make you feel?

You can also add: *Can we also eliminate things like 'think it over,' which usually means no, and ends up wasting your time?*

Again, be yourself and use your words, not mine. All you want to do is make the prospect feel comfortable with the idea that you may not be able to help them, that you are not there to sell them something they don't want or need. You are there to ask them questions to determine whether there is a fit or not and if not, you will tell them so, and/or it is ok for them to also tell you no, because you are ok with a no. But, you better be sure your attitude *is* ok with a no.

You have now set the parameters of working on an honest yes/no basis to which "think it over," one of a salesperson's biggest obstacles, no longer exists. The same process can work for you in eliminating common objections, interruptions and all other obstacles that you face in sales interactions or buyer encounters as I prefer to call them.

Dealing with common and major objections is one of the biggest fears of a salesperson. Most salespeople feel they have to justify, so they end up replying to objections. The best way to deal with a common objection is to deal with it right up front, in the setting up of the parameters. Simply take your most common or major objection and ask if it is going to be a problem.

For example,

By the way, we are the most expensive in the area. Is this going to be a problem?

If it is not a problem, move on. You just eliminated the objection (an excuse for not doing business with you) from coming up again.

If yes, understand fully what the objection fully means to the buyer, and find out why. Share case studies or third party stories to get the answer the buyer needs to overcome their own objection. They must solve their own objection, not you. You are there to guide them, by asking engaging questions, into discovering the answer for themselves, so that they own the solution, and feel empowered.

Engaging and empowering questions can be used in many ways to eliminate surprises and get buyer commitment.

For example, try this for getting a commitment on response times when communicating:

Salesperson: "For my reference, John, how do you like to be communicated with—telephone, fax, e-mail?

"If you were to leave a message for me, how quickly would you like me to respond?

"Can I expect the same from you in return?"

The same process applies to interruptions. Allow me to share a personal example how I overcame serious interruptions at a conference in Pakistan, where other speakers and I were speaking to over 400 business people. Fortunately, I was one of the last speakers to perform so I was able to witness the problem. I then realized I had to set the parameters and demonstrate how this simple technique can also work for the participants in the audience.

On day one of the conference there were three speakers on various topics, each speaking for 90 minutes. At the beginning of the conference, and after each speaker, the emcee would get up and tell everyone to turn off their cellular phones and beepers as it was disturbing others and causing interruptions. Nothing ever changed and the mobiles continued to sound off.

On day two the same thing happened. The emcee got up and asked everyone to turn off their mobiles. I was then introduced and began my talk on sales. I always like to open by asking questions to get to a point. The point I wanted to make with this audience was the importance of sales and it came across well. I then went into my overview of what I was going to cover over the next 90 minutes and asked how we can retain the information I was going to share with them. They answered the way I wanted them to: apply it within 48 hours, take notes, share it with others, etc.

Then I proceeded to eliminate the interruptions caused by mobiles. I walked off the stage down into the audience. I went up to a gentleman and asked him the following: *Have you ever been in the midst of a conversation where you are about to make an important point and the phone rings?* He answered yes, and I asked what happened. He replied that he lost his focus, his concentration. I then turned to another person somewhere behind me and asked him, *What can we do so that we don't lose our focus or concentration today?* He replied with "turn off our mobiles." "Great," I said, and then went to another person and asked if they agreed? She responded yes and I asked, *and if mobile goes off how should that person be penalized?* She replied with, "Have them take their call on stage. "I then ran up on stage and asked the full audience, *Is there anyone here who disagrees with the penalty—if your cellular or beeper sounds, you take the call on stage?* Not one hand went up, and guess what—not one cellular phone or beeper sounded during my presentation.

After my talk there was one more speaker. The emcee thanked the audience for turning off their mobiles and **told them** to keep them off. The emcee did not learn my technique. The audience was engaged in setting the parameters with me, and not the emcee or the next speaker. Unfortunately, the phones were ringing again.

Setting the parameters is a standard in all of my meetings and training sessions. It gives the participants ownership, not to mention involvement, engagement and empowerment, in the program. There is no particular order to setting up any of these parameters. Just make it a point to address the ones that matter most to you and your prospective buyer, and others as need be, in some way. Know what parameters you want to work under. Ask the right questions in a way that gets the other person to tell you what you want to hear. Remember that to have the parameters respected, it must be the other person's idea; they have to own it.

Summary

- Set the parameters by getting the prospective buyer involved, engaging them.
- Confirm time, objective, agenda, end result.
- Get permission to ask questions and to take notes.
- Make the buyer comfortable with saying "no" or "yes" and eliminate "think it over."
- Deal with major or common objections.
- Get commitment for communication response times.
- Deal with interruptions.

Uncovering Buying Motivators

What are buying motivators? Buying motivators are the reasons someone buys something. Your job as a salesperson is to uncover these reasons in advance so that you can facilitate the buying process for the buyer. Once you know the reasons, the rest is easy, but uncovering the reasons is easier said than done. First, let's understand why people buy.

People buy for emotional reasons. They justify their purchase intellectually. Features and benefits are not emotional and do not belong early in the sales process. There is a place for them and it is at the end of the process when you are providing a prescribed solution, step 3 of the Velocity Selling system, to a decision maker who is ready to make a buying decision. Therefore, stop those "feature and benefit" dumps. Your job at this stage of the process is to stay in control and qualify the prospect by uncovering their buying motivators.

There are two emotional reasons, *buying motivators*, why people buy something. One is to eliminate a pain and the other is to gain a pleasure. Which one of the two emotions do your products and/or services satisfy? Do they eliminate pain, do they provide a pleasure or do they fit into both categories?

If you sell real estate, you can be selling pain relief and/or pleasure depending on the buyer's needs. Pain relief is providing housing to someone who is desperately in need while pleasure could be selling in a prestigious resort community.

You have heard it before: no pain, no gain. This is true for sales; if you cannot find the prospect's pain, their emotional buying motivators, you will gain no sale. You can find someone's pain or pleasure by simply asking questions, questioning the answer and, of course, listening for cues. But first you must learn which questions to ask.

The best questions to ask to uncover buying motivators are those that can get a prospect talking openly about a topic that will identify problems, pains or pleasures to which you have solutions. Always start with an open-ended, yet leading or directing question in the area you want to go deep in.

The easiest way to do this is to create a three-column chart, like the one below, and in the "Solutions" column on the left, identify and list the solutions that your products or services provide. In the "Problems" column, list the emotional pains or pleasures that each solution solves. Then in the third column, "Topic questions," list the open-ended questions that need to be asked to uncover the problems to which you have solutions. There is no sense asking questions to uncover problems that you have no solutions for, is there?

Solutions	**Problems**	**Topic Questions**
1.	1. A.	1. A.
	B.	B.
	C.	C.
2.	2. A.	2. A.
	B.	B.
	C.	C.
3.	3. A.	3. A.
	B.	B.
	C.	C.

Being prepared in advance and knowing what questions to ask is half the battle. The other half is listening to the answers and questioning the answers to find out how bad the problem is or how bad the pain hurts. Before proceeding, make sure you complete the chart to the best of your ability.

Next, identify the information you need from each of the problems. These are the fact-finding types of questions you learned about in the earlier sections on asking questions. These are the answers you need that will help you qualify the buyer while positioning your solution to solve their problems.

Once you have gathered the factual information you need, you then need to dig a little deeper. You need to ask questions to get the buyer to analyze those problems in depth. Apply the rule of 3+. Question the answers. Also, ask questions such as:

How long have you had this problem?

What have you done to fix it?

Why hasn't it worked?

How much is this problem costing you or the organization?

How does this affect you?

How does this make you feel personally?

By asking these in-depth questions, you will be going deeper into the problem, deeper than most salespeople have ever gone before. Take a closer look at those questions. The answers can give you valuable information on timing, competition, what didn't work and why, how much the problem is costing the organization and what the real buying motivators are—both corporate and personal. At the same time you will be drawing out real personal emotions.

Personal emotions are what you have to draw out and where you have to get to. These are the strongest of all emotions. People will always solve their own problems before they solve someone else's. Find out the real personal problems and how it makes them feel and you will have a personal buying motivator in support of the corporate buying motivator. When you find out the personal buying motivators, your chances of success have just increased.

Once you have brought the buyer to realizing their personal buying motivators, reasons or pains, and how it makes them feel, don't dwell on it. Quickly move on to identifying other problems by asking another one of the open-ended questions you identified above to get them talking about other problems. Follow the process through again.

Once you have reviewed and identified three to five problems, you probably have enough information to determine if you have any buying motivators or not. If you do, proceed to the next step. If not, don't be afraid to abort. Remember, you set the parameter not to waste their time and to tell them you can't help them if you felt you couldn't. Respect what you agreed upon.

Again, this is not for you to tell, but to ask. Engage the buyer. Buyers need to uncover these things for themselves. That is what empowering the buyer is all about. You are there to guide them through the self-discovery process, not to tell them or make it simple for them. You should already know what talking too much will cost you.

I will see you in the next section on uncovering financial ability.

Summary

- Get and keep the buyer talking.
- Find the emotional problems or desires.

- Dig deep. Question the answer.
- Seek clarification and full understanding.
- Help the buyer find and feel the personal problem and associated costs.

Uncovering Financial Ability

Now that you have identified three to five buying motivators and believe that you can provide them with pain relief through your solutions, you have decided to proceed with the qualification process. The next step in the process is to identify the buyer's financial ability—if they have any money available, and how much, to solve the problems identified. This is also the step to question any and all financial issues that may be of concern.

A lot of people have problems talking about money because they were told that money is a personal matter and should never be discussed. Well, you are now in business and payment for a sale is important, is it not? If you don't discuss financial issues, how will you know what they can afford as a solution, or if your solution fits within their budget or if you will even get paid?

To enter into this step, using the buyer's words or language, simply review the problems, needs or issues identified in the previous step and ask the buyer this simple question:

Do you have a budget set aside to cover these issues?

Naturally they can answer yes or no. If they answer no, simply ask:

How do you intend to proceed? Shut up and wait for their answer, then question the answer and make a decision on how you want to proceed, whether to abort or whether to come back at a later date.

If they answered yes, simply ask: *Could you share that budget with me in round numbers?* "Sharing" is partnering and the use of "round numbers" is less intimidating. These two key words should always be used when uncovering financial ability. If the prospect provides you with the information you are looking for, great. However, if they answered: *Yes, but I can't share that information with you,* how would you respond?

Now you will have to revert to price ranges. For example, you could say something like: *Well, John, we have solutions in a variety of price ranges from $1,000 to $10,000. Would you be in the $1,000 to $5,000 range or the $5,000 to $10,000 range?*

Your job would be to narrow down the budget number to a point where you have some sort of idea of how much money is available to solve the problems. You can even ask questions on how they budgeted for similar purchases in the past.

Remember you are still gathering information, not giving it. However, if in the process you are forced to reveal your pricing, always reveal your highest price as it is easier to come down in price than it is to increase it later.

Also in the process you may uncover that there is not enough money in the budget to solve the client's problems or to pay for your solution. You will then have to make more decisions before moving on.

You can decide to take the little that there is and do something with it— service the client, build the relationship and be in a position to take it all when more funds are available. You can also reveal to the client that you cannot help them within the budget that is available. Whatever you decide to do, be open and honest as agreed and maintain the relationship.

You may have other financial issues that need to be dealt with: issues that relate to terms or methods of payment, for example. This is the time and place to discuss them. Don't leave any financial questions or issues on the table. Deal with them all now, by asking questions, not answering them!

Summary

- Review three to five problems identified.
- Ask "Have you got a budget set aside?"
- No: "How do you plan on proceeding?"
- Yes: "Would you mind sharing it with me in round numbers?"
- Use price ranges or bracketing.
- Question all necessary financial issues.

Uncovering Decision Making

You have now identified three to five buying motivators and discussed all financial issues. You know that there is a budget available and the approximate amount, and still believe that you can provide the client with pain relief within their budget. You have decided to proceed with the qualification process. The next step in the process is to uncover the buyer's decision-making process.

You start this step by using the buyer's words, reviewing the problems and budget you have already discussed, and simply ask: *John, when will a decision be made to solve these problems?*

"When" is one of the most important questions that need to be asked about making decisions. If the answer is now, great! But what if they don't know or what if they say in six months? What would you do then?

Hopefully you would remember to question their answers and get more in-depth information. I also hope you will realize that it is not wise to give a presentation until they are ready to make a decision. Why else would you give a presentation?

The other important question to ask is: *John, who besides yourself is involved in the decision-making process?* The important words here are "besides yourself." Quite often we think we are speaking with the decision maker, but in reality this person may only be able to say no. Your job is to uncover all people involved in the decision-making process. By including the individual you are speaking to, you are stroking them and making them feel important. Omit them and you are insulting them. Don't ever insult a buyer. By the way, you can also ask how similar decisions were made in the past, as history does repeat itself.

Should other people be involved, you have to find out who they are and go through the whole sales process again, with each decision maker, starting with building rapport. You will soon learn that everyone is different: different dominant senses, different buying motivators and even different budgets. You will have to appeal to them all, even if a committee is involved.

However, what can you do if you can't get in front of the committee? Well then you will need someone to represent you to that committee. You will have to uncover the questions that the committee would ask and then present and coach the individual that will be representing you. Make sure that person has as strong a belief in your solutions as you do.

Keep in mind that there could be many other people involved in influencing decisions too. These people could be consultants, agencies or even outside suppliers or friends. Find out who they are and if you can appeal to them as if they were decision makers as well. Follow the four-step "Buyer Focused" Velocity Selling System and remember that the more you know the better off you will be.

Summary

- Review problems and budget.
- Ask "When will you be making a decision?"
- Ask "Who *besides yourself* is involved in the decision-making process?"
- What about others: committees, agencies, etc.

Summarizing

You have built rapport with the buyer and established trust. You have now qualified the buyer on buying motivators, financial ability and decision making. You asked a lot of questions, listened effectively and empathetically to a lot of answers, questioned the answers and went deep. You remained in control of the process and have not revealed any significant information on your products and services. You are now in a position to review your findings with the buyer and to make a decision on the next step.

Before summarizing ask yourself the following questions:

1. Does the buyer have a need?
2. Are your products or services able to satisfy the buyer's need?
3. Is the buyer able to buy?
4. Is the buyer ready to buy?
5. Is the buyer willing to buy... *from you*?

Based on the answers to these questions you will have a good idea on where you stand in the sales process. You either have the potential of a sale or you don't. If you do, you continue to proceed with a presentation. If you don't, you consider your options on how you want to proceed: abort, refer the buyer to another supplier, or whatever. Whatever you decide to do, maintain the relationship for future development, introductions and referrals.

Let's pretend the buyer is qualified and you decide to proceed. There are two ways to summarize. One way is to ask the buyer to review what was discussed, to ensure clarification. The other is for you to review, or summarize, all of your findings. You identify the buying motivators, the budget allocated and the timing of the decision-making and the people involved. You then ask for confirmation of all of your summary findings.

It is important to note that you should be using the buyer's words and relating to the buyer's dominant sense at this stage of the process, not the words of the system or the words that you feel comfortable with. You have to be able to communicate with the buyer in the way they want to be communicated with. You also want to seek their confirmation on the buying motivators, budget and decision-making, or obtain any clarifications, before moving on.

You want to also uncover any other issues that could prevent you from doing business. After obtaining their confirmation on the summary simply ask,

Are there any other issues, problems or reasons that would prevent us from doing business?

If no, great! Proceed. If yes, find out what the issues, problems or reasons are, question the answer and proceed, or abort, accordingly. This is the time to defuse any bombs before they go off.

Next you want to move into the prescription phase, but first you want to reinforce one of the parameters set at the beginning of the meeting. The parameter is the yes/no decision. You could do that by saying something like,

John, at the beginning of our meeting we agreed to be honest with each other and to give yes/no answers. I believe I can solve your problems within your budget and timing. I am now prepared to provide you with a solution. At the end of my presentation are you still okay with giving me a yes or no answer?

You must receive a commitment here before you proceed. If you don't you could be wasting your time doing a presentation. Why would you even want to do a presentation if you are not going to get a yes or no answer?

Once you do get the commitment, you can also ask the buyer about their presentation expectations and the time that they can allocate to the presentation. You should also confirm the location of the presentation and the resources that may be needed.

All too often salespeople provide their canned presentation and dictate the time. Remember we are here for the buyer and without them, we have nothing. The presentation is for them, so that you can get a sale. Let's at least meet, or better still, exceed their presentation expectations. The only way we can do that is to ask and to prepare accordingly.

Remember that not all the steps in the sales process have to be completed at one meeting. Each meeting could be a step within itself or can run over several meetings depending on the complexity of the account. The important part is to continuously review your parameters and findings at each meeting, making the appropriate adjustments as need be. Constantly seek confirmation and clarification. When is doubt, don't proceed; question the doubt. You are the one in control of the process, are you not?

Join me in the next chapter on Prescribing Solutions.

Summary

- Summarize buying motivators, financial ability, decision making.
- Can you help the buyer or not?
- Confirm a yes/no response prior to presentation.
- Use the buyer's words and dominant sense.
- Ask for other issues or problems before proceeding.
- Know the buyer's presentation expectations and time allocated.

3. PRESCRIBING SOLUTIONS

Prescribed Presentations

You have built rapport and obtained the buyer's trust. You set the parameters; you uncovered the buying motivators, the financial ability and the decision-making process. You summarized your findings, obtained confirmation and got a commitment to proceed with a presentation to the decision makers, along with a commitment of a yes or no answer after the presentation. You now have a qualified buyer, or you would not be at this step in the process.

The objective of step 3, Prescribing Solutions, in the Velocity Selling System is to take everything you learned and to come up with a prescription: a customized solution based on your products and services, to solve the buyer's problems, within their budget and time frames.

This means you are to present solutions specific to the problems identified and no more. Your job is to now get the sale based on the information gathered. Sell today based on that information and get the sale. You can always go back and up-sell or cross-sell once you have the sale. For now stay focused on getting the sale by addressing solutions specific to the problems identified.

Here is the rule: Sell today, educate tomorrow!

To make this clearer, think about your last visit to a doctor. As a salesperson you are really no different. The doctor greets you and conducts a bit of small talk to make you feel comfortable. You do the same when you are building rapport with the buyer. The doctor tells you what he is going to do and then starts to ask you a lot of questions to identify the exact problem. You ask the buyer how they would like to proceed and you too start to ask a lot of questions to identify the exact problem. Once the doctor finds the problem, he summarizes the findings and usually provides you with a prescription to solve that specific problem. You are to do the same. When you ask the doctor about other issues, they usually book another meeting. You should do the same.

You are a professional, no different than a doctor, dentist or a lawyer. When you conduct yourself as a professional you gain respect. The respect of all buyers is what you should be aiming for. You do this by setting some professional standards for yourself and following them through.

Ask questions, listen, be honest, stay focused and develop relationships before you present.

This is the step in the Velocity Selling System where you do finally get to present. You get to present solutions to the problems, within the budget and time constraints that you uncovered, to the person or people who are ready and able to make a yes or no decision. This is the step where you will also let the buyer buy.

Presentation skills are a must for everyone, even if you are not in sales, as you must be able to present and sell yourself and your ideas to others. But before we get into the actual presentation we must realize that great presentations start with preparation. It is in the preparation where you can make a difference.

Preparation, when following the four-step "Buyer Focused" Velocity Selling System, started early in the process by gathering all the pertinent in-depth information, not just surface information. You even prepared in advance of the call and identified the questions to which you needed answers.

Too many salespeople don't prepare and don't dig deep enough before they present. They are impatient and anxious to get the sale and usually end up losing it because they didn't prepare to dig deep enough, listen or gather enough pertinent information—information that you now know is crucial if you are going to get the prospective buyer to buy your solution. The more information you can gather, the easier this preparation and presentation step will be for you.

When preparing for your prescribed presentation or proposal, consider all the information you gathered on audience physiology, tonality, words, dominant senses, parameters, buying motivators, finances, decisions, presentation expectations, resources and time allocated, etc. When doing a presentation or a proposal all of these elements have to be reviewed and confirmed, including the confirmation of a yes or no answer after the presentation, before providing your solution to the decision maker(s). That is why the previous step of summarizing is so important.

Let's also refer to this as the beginning of a presentation or proposal— a review of all of your findings to ensure nothing has changed while obtaining a confirmation of a yes or no answer at the end of the presentation.

Next we get into the second component of a presentation, the middle.

This is where your solutions come in. You have to decide on the solutions you will be providing to solve the specific problems identified—solutions that will not only solve the problems identified, but will solve them within the budget and time constraints. You also have to identify the features and benefits you will present and how you will present them in each participant's dominant sense, while exceeding their presentation expectations in the allocated time frame. This is the crucial step in a presentation. You have to demonstrate or prove how your products or services will solve their problems or give them the pleasures they are looking for.

In addition, you have to consider your opening and closing remarks. What can you say that will capture the attention of the individual or audience on opening? How will you close off? Don't be concerned about your closing remarks now, as that will be covered in the next section when we discuss how to let the buyer buy.

There are several ways to go about your opening remarks. You can open with a question or two relating to the solving of an identified problem, use a quote or simply state a relevant fact. Your opening statement should be powerful to capture their attention, and then followed with a greeting and an overview of what will be following. Tell them what you are going to do, so there are no surprises. Then you can begin your presentation.

Let's take a closer look at the presentation itself. You are prepared and you arrived earlier than scheduled. You set up, test equipment and greet everyone by shaking hands and matching their handshake as they arrive. You provide an opening statement, verbally greet them, provide an overview of how you are going to proceed with the presentation and confirm a yes or no answer at the end of the presentation.

You then proceed to review all the pertinent information you gathered and confirm nothing has changed. If things have changed, consider your options and react accordingly. Once confirmed, you proceed by asking a simple question like, *From the problems identified, which one would you like me to provide a solution to first?*

This technique invites the buyer to get involved. The answer you get will probably be their biggest problem. You then proceed to provide a solution to that problem. This is where all those features and benefits you have learned about your products and services come out, but mention only those that are relevant to the specific problem at hand.

Keep in mind that you are presenting to the decision maker(s) and you must be communicating to them is a way that is appealing to their dominant sense while using their words, tonality and physiology as best you can. You are there for them, not you, right?

The same applies to proposals. The main advantage you have when making proposals is to first deliver a proposal as a draft. A proposal follows the same lines as a presentation with the same beginning, middle and end. The difference is that the words are written, not spoken. The idea behind a draft proposal is to partner with a buyer. When you prepare a proposal and give it to someone, it has your ideas, not theirs, so you own it, not them. By getting their agreement to your submitting a draft proposal you are giving them a chance to provide input and take part-ownership. Your job is to ensure you get them to add, correct or adjust something in that proposal. As soon as they incorporate something into the proposal, they take ownership. The proposal goes from being "yours" to being "ours." It should be your objective to always partner with a buyer where possible.

Let's go back to the presentation. After presenting a solution to the buyer's biggest problem you want to obtain agreement as to its solution. You can do this by asking if this solution satisfies that problem. If you did your job right, the answer should be yes. You can then confirm that yes by asking, "100 percent?" Or, if doing a visual presentation, place a check mark next to that problem. If you get a no or not 100 percent, ask how it doesn't satisfy or what is missing. Ask questions to seek out what is missing or why they responded the way they did. If in doubt, take the blame as if you did something wrong and seek out where you went wrong. Resolve any and all issues relating to this problem and its solution before moving on. Once you get confirmation of 100 percent, move on by asking, *What problem would you like me to address next?*

You then proceed to provide solutions to that next problem using all the relevant product or service features and benefits and repeat the 100 percent confirmation process. If you have fewer than four problems to which you have to provide solutions, you may want to proceed to measure their interest. If you have more than four, continue this process until you feel the buyer is on board. If you are not sure how your presentation is being received, you can also proceed to measure their interest.

Measuring someone's interest can also save you time and get to the real issues. It is in the measuring process that we let the buyer buy.

Summary

- The purpose of a presentation is to get a sale.
- Always present in the other person's point of view and dominant sense.
- There are three parts of a presentation—beginning (summary), middle (solutions) and end (letting the customer buy).
- Open by getting their attention.
- Use your summary as the beginning and confirm nothing has changed.
- After the beginning ask: "Which problem would you like me to provide a solution for first?"
- Provide a solution to the problem within their budget and time frames.
- This is where the features and benefits of your products and/or services belong.
- Create draft proposals, which allow for partnering.

Let the Buyer Buy

The **Interest Technique** is a simple technique that you can use to measure the level of interest the buyer has in doing business with you by the way your solutions solve his or her problems. It can save time and reveal concerns or issues that may have been overlooked or not previously discussed. The interest technique also lets the buyer buy. Consider it as a trial close if you like, as it does lead to the close.

The interest technique is based on the common scale of 1 to 10 and should be presented in your words, keeping in mind the prospect's dominant sense. It could be something like this for a visual buyer: *On a scale of 1 to 10, where do you see yourself? One you don't see using our services, 10 you are already there seeing us as your supplier. Where do you see yourself on the scale?*

Naturally, you can get any number as a response. For a rating of under 6, you have to accept the blame, ask where you went wrong and use this information to take corrective action or take it as a lesson learned.

Mind you, if you followed the process from the beginning, asked the right questions, questioned the answers, dug deep, listened and are presenting prescribed solutions to the problems identified, within budget and time constraints, this should not be happening, right? But, if you did skip some of the steps in the process or did not dig deep enough, expect this to happen.

You should, however, be getting ratings above 7. Any rating between a 7 and a 9 is a good sign and warrants the question, *What will it take to get you to a 10?* Listen to their response and give them what it will take to get them to a 10. Then re-affirm their rating again. It should be a 10. If it is only a 9, have some fun and say something like *John, is it possible that you really work on a scale of 1 to 9 and 10 doesn't exist?*

Shut up and wait for their answer, which could be something like a simple giggle confirming you are right.

The buyer is now committed. All you have to do now is ask the closing question, which can be as simple as *What would you like me to do next?* Again, shut up and wait for a response. The buyer's response could be something like, "Let's complete the paper work, sign an agreement, or process the purchase order." Their response is where they buy.

If you followed and implemented the four-step "Buyer Focused" Velocity Selling System, you will experience how quickly you can qualify buyers, shorten your sales cycle, stay in control and experience this unbelievable and most rewarding phase of the process. There is no greater feeling that having someone buy from you through this self-discovery process.

But, it doesn't end here. You now have a client and that client has expectations of you, your organization and its products and services. You have to remain proactive, retain the account and develop it for more business.

I will see you in the next chapter.

Summary

- Use the Interest Technique: 1 to 10 scale, 1 no, 10 yes.
- Rating under 6: Take the fault, take corrective actions.
- Ratings 7 - 9: What must I do to get you to a 10?
- Close by asking: "What would you like me to do next?"
- Let the buyer buy.

Eliminating Potential Back Outs

You have gone through the process of converting a prospective buyer to a buyer. You now have a buyer who has agreed to purchase your products or service. You, or they, prepare all the paperwork and have it all signed off. However, you may have some concerns that you need to deal with—concerns about back outs or cancellations or how your competitor, from whom you are taking away business, will react. If you have any concerns about any of these details, or other issues, now is the time to address them.

Put yourself in the buyer's shoes. How do you feel after making a large purchase? Think about the last time you purchased a product or service of similar value to that which you are selling. Did you have any doubts about your purchase? Did you discuss it with others to re-affirm your purchase? Did you ever back out of a deal you made?

It is common for buyers to have what is called *buyer's remorse*, especially after purchasing large-ticket items. Is it possible that you, as a buyer, may experience buyer's remorse, consider backing out or turning back to your competitor, from whom you took the business, for a lower price or some other concession?

These are issues salespeople face on an ongoing basis. You have to be aware of these concerns and be able to address them now, while you are in front of the buyer, as you may not be able to get back in front of them once they back out. So, let's take a look at how we can deal with them one at a time.

If the client had to make a concession to do business with you and there is a possibility of a back out, select a minor concession or objection that might have come up somewhere in the process. Then ask if that concession, or any other issues, would cause them to back out of the deal. All you are trying to do is raise any issues that could lead to a back out while they are in front of you. If they don't raise any issues, you have their commitment that they wouldn't back out. If they do, deal with them immediately.

If you are taking business away from one of your competitors and are concerned that the buyer may go back to them, deal with it now, while you are in front of them. Simply ask them how they think your competitor, or their existing supplier, will react when they hear the news about you switching suppliers?

Ask the buyer what they think that supplier would do to keep the business or get it back? Ask them if they would go back? Address any issues in order to get their commitment to staying with you. You may want to provide the buyer with some coaching on how to deal with their existing supplier when they do call and offer lower prices or other concessions.

Think about the things you can do to add some extra value and build on the relationship you started. You may even volunteer to call their existing supplier and notify them for the client. Whatever you do, help the client however you can and get a commitment from them that they will respect and follow through on the agreement you made with them.

The next issue to cause back outs is buyer's remorse. Buyer's remorse usually sets in after the sale is made and you are gone. With buyer's remorse they go through three phases. First the buyer may experience some doubt and will then tell others of their purchase, looking for feedback, or external verification, as to whether or not they made the right decision. Based on all the feedback they obtained they will then proceed with the original decision or change their mind and cancel the sale. If you are selling products or services where buyer's remorse is an issue, again you must deal with it while the buyer is in front of you.

One of the best ways I have found to deal with buyer's remorse is to tell people third-party stories. Third-party stories help the client know about others like them that went through the same process as they did and what happened to them. They went home, told their friends, and their friends said... and then we got the call ... and they forgot why they made the purchase in the first place and the sale was reconfirmed.

Naturally, third-party stories have positive outcomes. Share those positive outcome stories with buyers that you think will go through buyer's remorse and ask them if it will be an issue or not with them. If so, deal with it then. If not, you have their commitment that it will not be an issue later.

With all of these issues, and others, you are just getting commitments by asking questions. In a way it is very similar to what you did when you set the parameters before starting the meeting. You have now set the parameters of what can happen, how to deal with it and how to proceed from this point on.

Now the buyer encounter is coming to an end. You must know the client's expectations and be prepared to exceed them. You should also ask for a referral or an introduction before leaving and let the buyer know when he or she will be hearing from you next. The sale is complete and you are leaving with commitments and referrals or introductions.

But first, before we complete the Prescribing Solutions chapter, you should learn how and why you need to ask for referrals. I will see you in the next section.

Summary

- Prevent back outs.
- Get commitment.
- Deal with the competition.

Asking for Referrals

A referral is asking a buyer or even an acquaintance for the name and contact information of someone who might have an interest, need or desire for your product or service. An introduction to the individual makes the referral even more powerful.

How do you get referrals and introductions? The answer is simple: **ASK!**

You already know that you have the right to ask. If you don't ask, you don't get. If you ask, you have a 50/50 chance of getting what you desire. However, don't despair if the information is not forthcoming. There is nothing lost as you cannot lose something you never had.

Simply make it a habit to ask everyone. Add it as a goal that you would like to accomplish on your Monthly Monitor Chart. You will no longer be making cold calls but instead you will work strictly on a referral basis.

Ask more to sell more! Don't miss out on this tremendous lead source!

The other option is word of mouth. You must always provide outstanding service and by doing so, others will talk about you in a very positive manner. You will find yourself in high demand. However, if you do not ask for testimonial letters or for referrals, the chances of receiving one out of the blue are slim.

You are given a referral because you have earned the other person's trust and they think you can actually help someone else. Do you believe in yourself? Do you want to help others? Do you trust yourself? If you don't, nobody else will either.

A referral allows you to introduce yourself by virtue of another person's good name. In doing so, you generate commonality and an immediate level of trust.

There are several reasons why you should ask for a referral. When you call a referral and encounter their voice mail, be sure to mention the name of the person who provided their name. The referral tends to respond faster and at a much higher rate compared to voice mails you leave by cold calling. A referral has an affinity with you that automatically produces an element of trust. Quite frankly, most people feel a sense of duty or obligation to those who referred their name. They feel compelled to call you back just in case they are asked about the referral. Either way, it works in your favor.

Referrals tend to listen intently and engage you more closely when you finally do reach them. Typically, they don't see you as "just another sales representative." A tentative bond is created in your mutual acquaintance. The referral is curious and wonders why his or her name was circulated. In simple terms, this gives you a significant edge.

Referrals tend to buy at a higher rate compared to those from cold calls and other lead sources.

There are three reasons for this outcome:

- People usually refer others who are in similar situations. They tend to have similar problems, concerns, needs, wants, and opportunities. This usually means there is a strong application for your product or service. In short, they are more qualified.

- As mentioned above, referrals tend to listen more closely to your message. They do not "dismiss" you as quickly or as lightly as they do other sales professionals.
- The referral's trust is typically elevated because he or she can "check you out." You have an instant credibility source. Every buyer is looking for someone they can trust and depend on. The evidence of success with a known acquaintance makes buying easier for a referral and easier for you.

Your selling cycle time is reduced simply due to trust. The time it takes the referral to buy is usually much less than any other lead source. This means less hassle and more sales.

As stated earlier, you can ask anyone for a referral. Existing buyers are the best referral source because they know you and they know your products or services. Never miss an opportunity to ask a satisfied buyer for a referral, and a testimonial letter while you are at it.

You can also ask prospective buyers. Suppose you call a prospective buyer only to discover that your product or service does not match his or her needs. You can still ask for a referral at the end of your call. What's the worst thing that can happen? They may say "no." No big deal. Move on. However, they just might provide you with a name. Now that's a great start.

Ask for referrals at the end of your visit or contact. Remember to do so AFTER you have completed your primary objective. Referrals seem easy enough but there is a certain amount of finesse required.

How you ask for a referral is also important.

Here's how **NOT** to ask for a referral:

Jim, do you know of anyone who might be interested in my services?

This is NOT the recommended approach because it is a closed-ended question making it far too easy for your buyer to say, *Ahh…no.* The "no" response is often impulsive in nature; an automatic response to a closed ended question. In other words, they respond negatively out of habit. You could be missing numerous opportunities.

The BETTER way to ask for the referral is:

Sandy, can you give me a name or two of someone you know who might be interested in these types of products?

The difference is subtle but significant. By asking for a "name," your client has to THINK about names. It is not quite as easy to give you a dismissive "no." Usually, they tend to do a mental scan of friends and associates. This scanning pause helps reduce the spontaneous "no" response. Of course, they can and sometimes will say "no" anyway. Nonetheless, by requesting a name you increase your odds and improve the chance for success.

One final point: referrals demonstrate good behavior. Make sure that those giving you referrals also get rewarded. Remember, any behavior that gets recognized or rewarded, gets repeated. Ask me about our referral reward program, if you are interested in referring others to us.

Summary

- ASK for referrals and/or introductions.
- A referral automatically produces an element of trust.
- Referrals tend to buy at a higher rate compared to those from cold calls and other lead sources.
- Your selling cycle time is reduced simply due to trust
- *Sandy, can you give me a name or two of someone you know who might be interested in these types of products?*
- Create a referral reward program. Remember, any behavior that gets recognized or rewarded, gets repeated.

4. MAINTAINING BUYER RELATIONSHIPS

Exceed Expectations While Providing Added Value

You now have to take the time to determine what steps to take next to maintain and develop the relationship you just started.

After you made a purchase, what are some of the things you would like to see happen? Sure you want your product or service delivered as scheduled, but what else? How can you exceed your buyer's expectations while providing them added value?

This is where you have the opportunity to stand out and make another significant difference. Come up with a list of things you can do that go beyond the verbal thank you. Show the client that you do appreciate their business, but go the extra mile for them, however you can. Think of ways to maintain the relationship, to stay in contact and to be considered as a friend or referred to as "my" supplier by your buyer. Don't think too much about it. Just do it!

Very few individuals take the five minutes it requires to acknowledge or thank someone with a personal handwritten note of recognition for their patronage. If you truly want to make your buyers or potential customers feel appreciated and special, then take the time to write and send a personal note. It may truly be the one extraordinary customer service step that brings the client back again and again.

There are numerous reasons that deserve to be acknowledged by a personal note, or even an e-mail message. Some of these are a purchase, a person taking the time to meet with you, a luncheon meeting, a presentation, a lead or a referral, a social or sporting event, a networking opportunity, and/or a gift. Make it a practice to show your appreciation and you will certainly make yourself memorable. When you exceed someone's expectations, you get more word of mouth and more referrals and introductions.

Make an effort to also stay in communications with the buyer. Follow up to ensure everything went according to plan. Always be proactive. Find reasons to continue communicating with them personally as well as for business. Go beyond what is standard or required, so that you become and remain the vendor of choice.

Think about the things you are striving to achieve. Are you working toward success at any cost, or are you adding value to others along the way? If you add value to others, they will value you in return and cheer for the successes you achieve in life.

Therefore, let's understand how salespeople can provide added value.

Value-added selling is a proactive philosophy of seeking ways to enhance, augment, or enlarge your bundled package solution for the buyer. It's promising a lot and delivering more, always looking for ways to exceed buyer expectations.

You can see that being proactive, exceeding customer expectations, being flexible and able to customize your approach are important. However, there are other elements that also provide added value, like being buyer focused, asking questions and listening effectively, solving problems, being accessible and responsive.

Initially, the value-added salesperson is a doctor—he diagnoses the buyer's problems and then prescribes the right solution.

Value-added salespeople define value in buyer terms, based on buyer needs, not seller terms or desires. When you define value in buyer terms, buyers pay for it with a higher selling price. Conversely, if you define value in your terms, you pay for it with a bigger discount.

Value, like beauty, is in the eye of the beholder. The salesperson's competence and attitude are primary drivers of customer satisfaction, loyalty and retention.

Value-added selling is substantially different from traditional selling:

- Traditional salespeople sell products. Value-added salespeople solve problems.
- Traditional salespeople attempt to create the buyer's needs. Value-added salespeople seek to understand the buyer's needs.

- Traditional salespeople make deals. Value-added salespeople want to create a long-term relationship and make a difference.
- The fundamental selling skill for traditional salespeople is closing.
- The fundamental selling skill for value-added salespeople is engaging: probing, listening and empowering the buyer to make decisions.

Here are some characteristics of value-added salespeople to conclude this chapter, and competency section.

- *Attitude.* The foundation of all successful people; a desire to be buyer focused.
- *Integrity.* Ninety-six percent of buyers say that the #1 thing they look for in salespeople is integrity. People want to do business with those whom they trust.
- *Empathy.* Empathy is the salesperson's ability to ask questions, listen, understand and view life from the buyer's point of view.
- *Initiative.* Having an owner's mentality and being proactive, one step ahead of the buyer; not waiting for someone to tell you what you must do.
- *Knowledgeable.* Buyers report that what they want most in a solution is to deal with salespeople who are knowledgeable, or experts in their field. If knowledge is power then what you don't know holds great power over you. Knowledge is empowerment.
- *Courage.* Courage is not the absence of fear—it's the management of fear. Value-added salespeople feel the fear and do what they know they must do.
- *Discipline.* Doing what you have to do, even when you don't want to do it.

Summary

- Show appreciation.
- Send personal handwritten notes.
- Maintain and develop the relationship for more business.
- Be proactive.
- Always look for ways to exceed buyer expectations.
- Define value in buyer terms, based on buyer needs.
- Value-added salespeople solve problems, seek to understand the buyer's needs and create long-term relationships.
- The fundamental selling skill for value-added salespeople is engaging: probing, listening and empowering the buyer to make decisions.

- Characteristics of value-added salespeople include: Attitude, Integrity, Empathy, Initiative, Knowledgeable, Courage, Disciplined.

Review and Daily Disciplines for Competencies: the "Buyer Focused" Velocity Selling System

In Competencies, Part 2, you learned the details of each step in the "Buyer Focused" Velocity Selling System.

You learned about building relationships and the importance of building rapport to establish trust. You learned about the NLP rapport pie and the importance of mirroring and matching physiology, tonality and words, as well as communicating in the buyer's dominant sense. In the process you also discovered your own dominant and secondary senses.

Now that you learned how to quickly establish rapport you moved on to step 2 of the Velocity Selling System: Qualifying Buyer Opportunities.

You learned how to engage the buyer to establish parameters, or set ground rules with the buyer, while focusing on their time allocation and objectives. You learned to ask permission to ask questions and take notes and you removed all possible barriers by making the buyer comfortable with no, and yes, while being honest with you. You learned how to deal with objections, interruptions and how to get communication commitments.

Next you learned how to uncover buying motivators by understating the pain and pleasure emotions and your prepared questions that would uncover those emotions to which you have solutions. From there you learned how to uncover financial ability and created questions to all possible answers. You also learned how to uncover decision-making and how to summarize all of your findings in order to proceed or abort, while maintaining the relationship.

You then moved on to step 3, Prescribing Solutions, where you learned how to prepare a prescribed presentation and let the buyer buy using the interest technique. You learned how to eliminate back outs from buyer's remorse to taking the business from your competitor and developed strategies accordingly. Finally you learned how and why you should ask for referrals.

In the final step of the Velocity Selling System, step 4, Maintaining Buyer Relationships, you learned how to show buyer appreciation and how to exceed their expectations while providing added value.

You learned a lot here and you will soon be rewarded for your efforts. All that is left to do is for you to reflect on all of the learning you received through the notes you took. It is now time to go to your notebook and write out the daily disciplines you want to instil in your life and then do what you have to do. Remember that any behavior that gets recognized or rewarded gets repeated, so include them as well.

Daily Disciplines: **Competencies: the "Buyer Focused" Velocity Selling System** Part 2

What did you learn?

___

___

___

___

1. What daily disciplines do you want to apply for yourself?

___

___

___

___

What will your reward be for doing what you say you will do?

___

___

___

___

2. What daily disciplines do you want to apply toward your Organization?

___

___

___

___

What will your reward be for doing what you say you will do?

___

___

3. What daily disciplines do you want to apply toward buyers?

___

___

___

___

What will your reward be for doing what you say you will do?

____

____

____

____

Reminder: review these disciplines daily for the next twenty-one consecutive days, or using the Monthly Monitor Chart for twenty-five out of thirty-one days and you will make these disciplines effective habits.

DISCIPLINE: DOING WHAT YOU HAVE TO DO

Discipline Toward Yourself

Discipline Toward Your Organization

Discipline Toward Your Buyers

DISCIPLINE TOWARD YOURSELF

What is discipline? Does discipline have anything to do with success or motivation? Does discipline have anything to do with your everyday life? Can discipline be an effective habit? Is discipline necessary to succeed in sales?

Discipline is defined as a commitment to the most important person in the world—**YOU**. It means doing what you have to do, even when you don't want to do it.

Discipline is an effective habit and effective habits lead to effective results. Conversely, ineffective habits produce ineffective results. Firstly, you must discipline yourself to seek awareness and rid yourself of ineffective habits. Then, by using discipline, replace those ineffective habits with useful and productive ones. By doing so, you can achieve anything you want in life.

Discipline, along with a positive attitude, is within your control. Don't allow those ineffective habits to control you and your future. Instead, discover how daily discipline will eventually alter any negative habits and change your life for the better. Go ahead and make the decision to lead a disciplined life and reap the benefits.

Discipline is an effective habit. Discipline is a complete process that includes personal awareness, desire, determination, recognition and reward.

Personal behavior is a part of discipline. Once a meticulous behavior is recognized and rewarded, it gets repeated. The process is simple. You determine the necessary behavior or action required to achieve the goal, do it even when you don't want to; and finally, recognize and reward that behavior so it will be repeated. If not, penalize yourself by not getting that reward.

Allow me to tell you more about the discipline in my life, the "Bob time" discipline, which is really just "me" time.

As I shared early on in The Understanding of Four Key Words, the Bob time discipline is dedicating at least one hour of my most productive time in the day to the most important person in the world, myself.

What is your most productive time of your day? Is it early morning, day or night?

In my case, it is the morning. When I realized this years ago, I changed my wake up habits. In the past I would get up at 7a.m. and have a coffee. Now I wake up at 6 a.m. and I dedicate the first hour of my day to myself. I labelled that most powerful hour Bob time.

During Bob time, I accomplish things that will help Bob get where Bob wants to go. You might say there is plenty of *Bobbing* going on. The focus is solely on me. Firstly I give to myself so that I may give to others.

When Bob time is over, I reward myself with a cup of coffee. This is one example of how to make discipline part of your life. Any behavior that gets recognized and/ or rewarded gets repeated. If you do what you say you are going to do, then reward yourself for doing it and this accomplishment will get repeated.

That first coffee certainly tastes great at 7 a.m., especially now that it is my reward for completing what I was committed to do. But it doesn't end there. While drinking that cup of coffee, I give gratitude for being able to have a cup of coffee when there are millions of people around the world who cannot get a clean cup of water to drink.

After my cup of coffee, I exercise between 7 and 8 a.m. as I believe in physical fitness. What do you think my reward is at 8 a.m.? If you happened to say breakfast, you are right. Another opportunity to show my gratitude when there are kids in our own neighborhoods going to school hungry each day.

Then, between 8 and 9 a.m., I shower and get ready for a seminar. How do you think I feel now when I stand on stage? How effective a trainer or speaker will I be?

If I don't give to myself first, I can't give to others what I have inside to give. I won't be able to present effectively to the seminar participants. Unless I maintain personal discipline in my daily routine, I won't feel productive nor will I be able to engage others to introduce discipline into their own lives.

Remember, any behavior that gets recognized and rewarded gets repeated. However, if you did not do what you said you were going to do, you must do without the reward. That is the punishment, so make sure your rewards are simple, yet worthy and enjoyable as my first cup of coffee is.

What if you were to dedicate one hour of your most productive time daily to the most important person in the world... how would your life improve? How much more would you enjoy life? How much more would you appreciate the little things that you have taken for granted, such as coffee and breakfast?

Bob time is both my discipline and an effective habit.

Statistics stipulate it takes twenty-one days to develop a habit. Rest assured that my Bob time discipline and subsequent reward is a definite habit. And that first cup of coffee tastes better than ever before.

Take the time to reflect on your most productive time of day. Once you determine that time, fully use one hour of your most productive time and reward yourself upon completion, or punish yourself accordingly. In no time, you will be disciplined and will achieve the things you thought were impossible in your life.

Throughout this book we have provided you with all sorts of tools and we ended each category with a review and daily disciplines. You have had the opportunity to identify those daily disciplines that you need to put into action in each of the three previous courses. Now it is the time to gather them all and summarize them into your one daily discipline form. Once complete, prioritize them and add them into your Monthly Monitor Chart so that you can monitor yourself on your daily disciplines, and make them your effective habits.

Take the time now to summarize all the daily, weekly and monthly disciplines you desire for yourself. When done join me in the next chapter on discipline toward your organization.

Realize that you are the most important person in the world and that you need to take care of yourself first, and everything else revolves around you and your belief, attitude and behaviors toward yourself.

Here are some guidelines to help you establish additional disciplines toward yourself:

... What do you believe about you and how do you feel today?

... What will you do to have a win-win owner's mentality?

... What is the most productive time of your day?

... What will you do during that time that will give you the best ROTI?

... Define your daily, weekly and / or monthly disciplines.

… If you do what you say you are going to do, what is your daily, weekly or monthly reward?

… If you don't do what you say you are going to do, what is the punishment?

My Daily Disciplines	*The Reward for Doing*	*The Punishment for NOT Doing*
1.		
2.		
3.		
4.		
5.		
6.		
7.		
8.		
9.		
10.		

My Weekly Disciplines	*The Reward for Doing*	*The Punishment for NOT Doing*
1.		
2.		
3.		
4.		

5.

6.

7.

8.

9.

10.

My Monthly Disciplines	*The Reward for Doing*	*The Punishment for NOT Doing*
1.		
2.		
3.		
4.		
5.		
6.		
7.		
8.		
9.		
10.		

DISCIPLINE TOWARD YOUR ORGANIZATION

You realize why you are motivated about going to work and how each day brings you a day closer to the realization of your dreams. What daily disciplines do you need to apply toward reaching your sales success and organizational goals?

Primarily, to increase sales we need to establish a benchmark.

Do you know your sales process numbers as discussed in an earlier chapter? For example, your sales call-to-close ratio? Yes ___ No ___

If you answered YES, you are using discipline to inflate increased sales. You should be aware of your daily disciplines, what you have to do daily to increase sales results and the basis of these results. If not, look intently at how you got those results. They will identify the proper disciplines required to increase sales.

If your answer is NO, you lack discipline and must begin tracking your daily behavior as discussed in the earlier chapter on behavior toward your organization. This includes your sales disciplines especially if you yearn to increase sales. Make note of or track what you habitually do daily to increase sales.

You can track your daily disciplines by creating an uncomplicated form as discussed in an earlier chapter. Simply completing this form is a discipline.

By tracking your daily sales disciplines (activities), totaling these disciplines at the end of the month and averaging all disciplines, you will soon learn what we in the sales profession call your sales call-to-close ratio in regards to increasing sales.

By now you should know your numbers. Can you define the daily sales disciplines and activities that are essential to increase your sales?

It is purely a matter of discipline and doing what you say you will do, even if you don't feel like doing it. Discipline is the key to increased sales.

Remember, attitude and discipline are both within your control. They are the foundation for ongoing self-motivation and personal success. Recognize and reward appropriate behaviors and you will enjoy effective habits and valuable disciplines. You will be well on your way to where you want to go.

Now, define the daily sales disciplines and activities that are essential to increase your sales and meet your organizational objectives.

Go back to your daily disciplines noted at the end of each of the previous three chapters and summarize the disciplines toward your organization here.

Here are some guidelines to help you establish additional disciplines toward your organization

... What do you believe about your organization and why are you going to work?
... When is pay time and no-pay time?
... What are you daily / weekly pay-time behaviors?
... What will you do daily that will give you the best ROTI?
... What are you doing to increase your call-to-close ratio?
... What will you do to continue attract buyers?
... If you do what you say you are going to do, what is your reward?
... If you don't do what you say you are going to do, what is the punishment?

My Daily Disciplines	*The Reward for Doing*	*The Punishment for NOT Doing*
1.		
2.		
3.		
4.		

5.

6.

7.

8.

9.

10.

My Weekly Disciplines	*The Reward for Doing*	*The Punishment for NOT Doing*
1.		
2.		
3.		
4.		
5.		
6.		
7.		
8.		
9.		
10.		

My Monthly Disciplines	*The Reward for Doing*	*The Punishment for NOT Doing*
1.		
2.		
3.		
4.		
5.		
6.		
7.		
8.		
9.		
10.		

DISCIPLINE TOWARD YOUR BUYERS

You defined the perception you want from buyers and are acting it out. You conduct the appropriate pay time and no-pay time behaviors, and you always strive for the best ROTI. You attract, engage and empower buyers to buy. What daily disciplines do you need to practice toward buyers to ensure the above become real?

In earlier chapters you learned about buyer perceptions and how you can change your attitude and behaviors in order for those perceptions to become a reality.

You learned how to attract buyers by creating a personal marketing plan and positioning yourself as an expert in the marketplace. You also identified ways of getting the best ROTI, how to retain buyers, regain lost buyers and how to gain new buyers. All of these are disciplines within themselves.

To stay on top of your game, you need to create and apply daily, weekly and monthly disciplines. The choice of disciplines that you want to instill toward yourself, your organization or toward buyers is your own. Only you can make that choice and only you can make that difference.

Remember that any behavior that get recognized or rewarded gets repeated. Therefore, take the time to recognize and reward yourself for doing what you said you would do, and punish yourself accordingly if you don't. Follow this path for twenty-one consecutive days or twenty-five out of thirty days on the Monthly Monitor Chart and your daily disciplines will become an everlasting effective habit. Discipline will become an integral part of your life.

A Chinese proverb says "*To know and not to do, is not to know.*"

You now know what you have to do. Now it is up to you to do what you have to do.

Go back to your daily disciplines noted at the end of each of the previous three categories and summarize the disciplines toward your buyers here.

When done, join me in the final chapter, Conclusion. Congratulations!

Here are some guidelines to help you establish additional disciplines toward your buyers

... Do you believe there are buyers waiting to buy from you?

... When a buyer is in front of you, who is the most important person in the world?

... What will you do to engage and empower the buyer to buy?

... How will you gain and maintain the buyer's trust and relationship?

... How will you make the buyer feel they are in control, while you remain in control?

... What will you do during the time you have with buyers that will give you the best ROTI?

... If you do what you say you are going to do, what is your reward?

... If you don't do what you say you are going to do, what is the punishment?

My Daily Disciplines	*The Reward for Doing*	*The Punishment for NOT Doing*
1.		
2.		
3.		
4.		
5.		

6.

7.

8.

9.

10.

My Weekly Disciplines	*The Reward for Doing*	*The Punishment for NOT Doing*
1.		
2.		
3.		
4.		
5.		
6.		
7.		
8.		
9.		
10.		

My Monthly Disciplines	*The Reward for Doing*	*The Punishment for NOT Doing*
1.		
2.		
3.		
4.		
5.		
6.		
7.		
8.		
9.		
10.		

THE STEP-BY-STEP "BUYER FOCUSED" VELOCITY SELLING SYSTEM REFERENCE SUMMARY AND POST-CALL REVIEW

1. Build Rapport:

Find commonality
Mirror and match physiology, tonality, words
Open-ended question; listen
Determine visual, auditory or kinesthetic

2. Set Parameters:

Time, objective, agenda, end result/outcome, yes/no, permission to ask questions/ take notes, interruptions and biggest objection

3. Buying Motivators:

Dig deep, the 80/20 rule
For how long has the problem existed?
What have they done to fix it?
Why hasn't it worked?
How much is it costing them or their organization?
How does it make them feel personally?

4. Financial Ability:

Review three or four identified problems
"Have you got a budget set aside?"
No: how do they plan on proceeding?
Yes: "sharing" and "round numbers"
Use price ranges, bracketing

5. Decision Making:

Review of problems and budget
"When will you be making a decision?"
"Who besides yourself" is involved in the decision-making process? Committees, agencies, etc. factor

6. Summarizing:

Buying motivators, financial ability, decision making
Confirm a yes /no response prior to presentation
In the buyer's words and dominant sense
Ask for other issues or problems before proceeding
Know the buyer's presentation expectations

7. Prescribing Solutions:

Prescriptions; sell today, educate tomorrow
Client's point of view (dominant sense)
Beginning (summary): confirm nothing has changed
Middle (solutions): features & benefits (draft proposals)
"Which problem would you like me to provide a solution for first?"
Interest Technique: 1 to 10 scale, 1=no, 10=yes
Rating under 6: Take the fault
Ratings 7 to 9: What must I do to get you to a 10?
End: Letting the buyer buy
"What would you like me to do next?"

8. Maintain the Relationship:

Follow up / Buyer's Remorse,
Show appreciation
Ask for referrals/introductions
Be proactive

ABOUT THE AUTHOR

Bob Urichuck is an internationally renowned Velocity Selling Specialist. With over forty-five years of sales experience, ranging from door-to-door sales to corporate high-value boardroom sales, he has accumulated a wealth of experience in selling to individuals and big corporations.

For the last fifteen years, he has inspired, educated and empowered Fortune 500 companies and mid-sized businesses to increase the velocity of their sales and the strength of their bottom lines.

Using Singapore, Dubai and Ottawa as his ongoing hubs, Bob has spoken in more than 1,500 cities in over forty-five countries to audiences of up to 10,000 people.

Bob has been recognized as Consummate Speaker of the year and ranked #4 in the World's Top 30 Sales Gurus.

He is a Certified Sales Professional, Certified Master Trainer and Certified Social Entrepreneur who has adopted a village in Sri Lanka where he is financially responsible for the medical care and education of over 700 children who survived the deadly tsunami of 2004.

Bob is an International Professional Speaker, Trainer and Author of two best-selling books *"Up Your Bottom Line"* and *"Disciplined for Life: You are the Author of Your Future."*

Want Sales Training or a Conference Keynote Speaker?

Bob's RESULTS-oriented approach means that he takes the time to truly understand your needs and those of your conference audience or training participants. When you hire Bob, he delivers a custom-designed program, not a "canned" presentation or training program. Using a myriad of proven, interactive adult learning techniques, Bob propels both the team and the individual to commit to actions that lead to measurable results. Combine this with Bob's partnership approach to continuous learning and reinforcement, and you are guaranteed lasting results.

Contact Information:
Bob Urichuck
Bob Urichuck Management Inc
86 Gilchrist Ave
Ottawa, Ontario
K1Y 0M8
Canada
Tel: (819) 827-2296 Toll Free: 1-877-658-8224
Fax: (819) 827-1658
E-Mail: bob@bobu.com
Web: http://www.BobU.com
http://www.velocityselling.com/

Sales Velocity. Your Bottom Line. Our Passion.

BIBLIOGRAPHY

Batchelor, David J. *Skills for Sales Success.* Toronto: Canadian Professional Sales Association, 2000.

Covey, Stephen. *The Seven Habits of Highly Effective People.* New York: Simon and Schuster, 1989.

Domanski, James. *Profiting by Phone - No Nonsense Skills and Techniques for Selling and Getting Leads by Telephone.* Omaha. Business By Phone Inc., 1997.

Harvey, Christine. *Secrets of the World's Top Sales Performers.* Arrow Books, 1991.

Girard, Joe. *How to Anything to Anybody.* New York: Warner Books, 1977.

Girard, Joe. *How to Sell Yourself.* New York: Warner Books, 1981.

Gleeson, Kerry. *The Personal Efficiency Program.* New York: John Wiley & Sons, Inc., 1994.

Hill, Napoleon. *The Law of Success.* Chicago: Success Unlimited, Inc., 1979.

Hill, Napoleon. *The Think and Grow Rich Action Pack.* New York: Hawthorn Books Inc., 1972.

Lakin, Alan. *How to Get Control of Your Time and Your Life.* New York: The New American Library, Inc., 1973.

Mandino, Og. *The Greatest Salesman in the World.* New York: Bantam, 1983.

Miller, Robert B.; Heiman, Stephen E. *Strategic Selling.* New York: Warner Books, Inc. 1985.

Sandler, David H. *You Can't Teach a Kid to Ride a Bike at a Seminar.* New York: Dutton, 1995.

Urichuck, Bob. *Disciplined for Life: You Are the Author of Your Future.* Ottawa: Creative Bound, 2008.

VELOCITY SELLING VIRTUAL TRAINING

VelocitySelling.com—an innovative web-based learning platform that provides corporate sales professionals, small business owners and entrepreneurs with a step-by-step sales process that will put them in control of the sales process, shorten sales cycles, and increase their ROTI (return on time invested), margins and revenues.

The virtual training platform, engineered by Lightspeed VT, provides a comprehensive range of corporate training and communication measurements for management: monitoring, tracking, testing and reporting on each individual's performance and results within corporate teams. It can be used in head offices and branches world-wide, and offers an interactive, virtual format that is as engaging as it is innovative.

Within the training system, there are four main learning categories and more than 350 modules of interactive video, from thirty seconds to seven minutes in length, supported by workbooks, assignments, real life application, and testing. Using interactive learning techniques participants will quickly be able to apply their learning in the real world and master Urichuck's non-traditional buyer-focused sales techniques in bite-sized portions.

The online sales training programs are affordable and accessible twenty-four hours a day and the material is comprehensive; it will take a trainee more than a year to fully complete all modules. This allows learning to become an ongoing process that can be integrated effectively, unlike the learning from most two-day motivational sales workshops.

Upon completion of the sales training, participants will be recognized as "Buyer Focused" Velocity Selling System ambassadors and receive certification personally endorsed by Bob. Train-the-Trainer certification is also available.

Free Password to Interactive Virtual Training System

Thank you for purchasing *Velocity Selling, How to Attract, Engage and Empower Buyers to Buy*. For additional learning support, and for a limited time period, you can claim your free password to the Velocity Selling interactive video virtual training system by visiting

http://www.velocityselling.com/book

Looking forward to sharing more learning with you on the inside. Bob

Sales Velocity. Your Bottom Line. Our Passion

THE SALESMAN'S PRAYER

Oh creator of all things, help me. For this day I go out into the world naked and alone, and without your hand to guide me I will wander far from the path which leads to success and happiness.

I ask not for gold or garments or even opportunities equal to my ability; instead, guide me so that I may acquire ability equal to my opportunities.

You have taught the lion and the eagle how to hunt and prosper with teeth and claw. Teach me how to hunt with words and prosper with love so that I may be a lion among men and an eagle in the marketplace.

Help me to remain humble through obstacles and failures; yet hide not from mine eyes the prize that will come with victory.

Assign me tasks to which others have failed; yet guide me to pluck the seeds of success from their failures. Confront me with fears that will temper my spirit; yet endow me with courage to laugh at my misgivings.

Spare me sufficient days to reach my goals; yet help me to live this day as though it be my last.

Guide me in my words that they may bear fruit; yet silence me from gossip that be maligned.

Discipline me in the habit of trying and trying again; yet show me the way to make use of the law of averages. Favor me with alertness to recognize opportunity; yet endow me with patience which will concentrate my strength.

Bathe me in good habits that the bad ones may drown; yet grant me compassion for weakness in others. Suffer me to know that all things shall pass; yet help me to count my blessings of today.

Expose me to hate so it not be a stranger; yet fill my cup with love to turn strangers into friends

But all these things be only if they will. I am a small and a lonely grape clutching the vine yet thou hast made me different from all others. Verily, there must be a special place for me. Guide me. Help me. Show me the way.

Let me become all you planned for me when my seed was planted and selected by you to sprout in the vineyard of the world.

Help this humble salesman. Guide me, God.

Og Mandino
The Greatest Salesman in the World
New York: Bantam, 1983

www.ingramcontent.com/pod-product-compliance
Lightning Source LLC
Jackson TN
JSHW021411170426
101040JS00013B/199
9781614488170